A Home Vegetable Garden

Suggestions of Real Gardens for Homemakers and Others

Ella Mary Freeman

APPLEWOOD BOOKS
Bedford, Massachusetts

A Home Vegetable Garden
was originally published in

1922

9781429014083

Prepared for publishing by HP

The Open Country Books—No. 2

A HOME
VEGETABLE-GARDEN

*Suggestions of Real Gardens for Home-
Makers and Others*

BY

ELLA M. FREEMAN

𝔑𝔢𝔴 𝔜𝔬𝔯𝔨

THE MACMILLAN COMPANY

1922

COPYRIGHT, 1922,
BY THE MACMILLAN COMPANY.

Set up and electrotyped. Published October, 1922.

Press of
J. J. Little & Ives Company
New York, U. S. A.

CONTENTS

CONTENTS

A HOME
VEGETABLE-GARDEN

I

THE JOY OF A GARDEN

You ought to own a garden. Size does not matter particularly, and it is not necessary that you hold a legal deed to your garden. Once you dig the soil yourself and sow the seed yourself; once your own plants begin to grow and to thrive under your care—your own work in weeding and watering—then the garden is yours and all the beauty around is yours. The sweet scents and the bird songs; the shadow on the hillside and the sound of the breeze in the trees—all are yours. As Titbottom says, "you own the landscape when you work a garden."

I own my garden,—the vegetables that grow there and the cuckoo in the shelter of the low boughs of an old apple tree on its edge. Lavender and English thyme and sweetest fennel grow by the garden walk; and every morning on my way to work I am refreshed by the whiffs of herby fra-

1

grance. Farther down the path are sweet williams
and harebells and spicy grass pinks and forget-
me-nots. At its time of bloom, the long broad
row of lemon lilies floods the flower strip with
its golden fragrance. The old-time roses of gen-
erations gone by are rich with blossoms in their
turn. Early in the spring, the little "star of
Bethlehem" shines pure white the whole length
of the grass-grown walk. There are "pineys" of
the old days and the hollyhocks so rich and tall.
Most of the flowers our grandmothers loved make
beautiful the flower strip between the house and
the garden plot; and every morning, the whole
season through, some flower has a message in color
and fragrance. I own all the flowers in the garden and they all bloom for me.

Always the robins, my robins, are waiting for
me. They follow my hoe and watch for the worms
and the bugs as I work. The goldfinches sing to
me early and late, as they make their dipping flight
from the garden border to the orchard beyond.
There in the high old trees, the flicker calls to his
mate. Close at hand, in the nearest tree, the cat-
bird scolds. The song sparrow builds her nest
in a low raspberry bush. Then, while she tends
the home, her mate sits on the orchard fence and
sings and sings and sings. I own all the birds in
my garden and they all sing for me.

I grow beets and beans and carrots and corn.
Of course, I work hard and tend them with care

for I grow them to eat; but life is more than meat, and it is not all of gardening to grow things to eat. One learns to look at the plants as they grow. In time, one learns to see what mean beauty of leaf and blossom, grace of form and growth, and the marvel of color in growing things. Have you ever really looked clear into the heart of a big squash blossom? I once found there a bumble-bee trying to balance his clumsy body, while he reached for the sweets so far from him below. I held my face close and the broad sheltering squash leaves shut out the sunlight, leaving a mellow golden twilight in the big bell-like blossom.

Do you know how fragrant a cucumber blossom is? So fragrant, it fills its place in the garden full of perfume, when the dew forms at night. The big clumsy martynia grows scores of exquisite orchid-like blooms. The okra blossom has colors as rich and varied as those of the choicest gladioli. Garden peas are as pretty as sweet peas. Blossom and fruit; bird song and sunlight and cool shade; the fresh odor of the newly turned soil; the continual surprises and the wonder of growth—these are some of the riches of a real gardener.

Will you adventure with me? Will you set out to be a real gardener? Then let us talk together about how to work a garden in this real way, successfully. The piece of ground will be secured somehow or other. It does not matter how, so you have it. You will get it broken up, prepared

—by spade or plow—somehow. That is not important. The seeds you must select and put in with care and patience yourself. I count that really important. Now you must work it yourself, work it thoroughly. The amount of work your garden needs will depend on you rather than on the weeds.

The almanac will not help you. The clock will be of little use. Let me tell you when to work. In the morning early, if your head feels heavy and the day's work seems too much for you; if your confidence is low, your courage gone; if you trust your friend a little less, suspect your neighbor, doubt the good,—why, that's just the time to work your garden. And, mark me! work it hard, in the place that needs you most; and always turn your back upon the house,—the world. Perhaps, after dinner, when the meal is over, you will need to go at it again. Then it may be best to remember that the bugs are on the cucumber vines and the May beetle grubs are eating the strawberry plants. There are shady places in the garden at noon, and there is always plenty that needs to be done. You will know when to work; and you will know when to neglect your garden.

When your courage is high and your nerve is steady, when you can laugh with life, then you may let the weeds grow. It cannot hurt much. Mother nature is a "steady hand." She works early and late and plods on patiently, keeping at it in spite of insects and drought, against all odds, and with a skill no gardener can match. You will keep at it too, for the interest grips one and grows as one works. Finally, when fall and bonfire time come around, you will wonder at your great possessions, how many and how varied they are.

II

GARDENING AGAINST ODDS

It was certainly gardening against odds in 19—. It was the testing of a summer of drought. No country woman in New York state needs to be reminded of the late spring frosts of that year; of the long drought that followed; of the hard killing frosts in the early fall. As country gardeners, we have not forgotten the disappointment on finding our carefully tended early plants burned by the frost, in spite of the care we had taken. We remember how we fought the drought, and the bugs and the lice as well. We do not easily forget the day before and the day after the big fall frost. The day before, we were feeling proud of what—in very spite of Nature's biggest obstacles—had finally been accomplished. Lima bean poles were loaded to the top; the tomato plants were rich in their burden of big red fruit; the tiny bush melons even were ripening; the corn that with regular corn persistence had come on in spite of frost and drought, was bending with its load of ears. The day after the frost? Well, the vision still held. The testing, we had faced with joy. You see, we real gardeners had

6

put into our gardens—yes,—good seed and hard work; but we had put in other things as well: all our hopes and memories of gardening years gone by; all the bird songs we had heard; all the nests we had found; all the flowers; all their fragrance. In spite of the drought, the flicker still called just as clearly as ever in the big old orchard trees. The goldfinches sang as always before; and the white clouds floated by, their hillside shadows even more distinct. The song sparrows thrived lustily in their nests in the dry clover sod close by the garden's edge. All the old bird friends were there—and some new ones too. The whole summer through, the ruby-throated humming birds hovered over the flower strip and among the vegetable blossoms. The dry weather made the color of the flowers richer, the fragrance of the herbs greater. Then we put into our gardens, that summer, a love for the game of gardening won through other years of practice. The unusual difficulties made gardening more worth while. Hard work was more fun than ever; the rest in the shade of the trees as refreshing. And the real gardeners won out, every one, in most practical fashion. All summer long, there were plenty of fresh vegetables for cooking and for the tenderest salads; and, besides, plenty to can for the winter's supply. Through all the testing, all the difficulties of the summer of the drought, the vision grew for the real gardener.

In making a practical estimate of the results of
this dry-farming garden, the price considered was
the average retail price that would have been paid
to the grocer, had the fruit and vegetables been
purchased; and these rates were, of course, be-
fore-the-war prices. Expenses are considered
only in part. The gardener's labor is not in-
cluded, because it was a labor of joy and brought
great returns in health.

Let us turn the expense of labor toward the
balance of the real gardener's glorious profit.
Labor paid for amounted to $6.51. The plowing
and general preparation of the garden was done
by the hired man and the farm team at off hours.
For seeds $3.10 was paid; $2.00, for commercial
fertilizer. Other fertilizers came from the farm
supply. The total of money paid out was $11.61,
leaving a money profit, on paper, of $73.60. It
seems only fair to consider the special handicaps
of that particular year. The late spring frost
of June 8th burned the strawberries, corn,
all unprotected currants and gooseberries, the
grapes and asparagus, even the First-of-All
peas. The drought nearly destroyed the summer
squashes, ruined the cucumbers, and finally because of slow development nearly spoiled the
winter squashes. The early fall frost of September 12th came when many vegetables had not
reached their best. Nearly three dozen winter
squashes would have matured, in spite of the

drought, had there been the usual time. Only two pickings of lima beans had been made. The latest sown snap beans were loaded. The tomato crop was just beginning to be harvested. More than three dozen melons were nearly ready to ripen. The okra was blossoming full and pods forming rapidly. Even the lentils, grown for the first time, were blossoming well and making pods. The garden was full of promise of a big fall fruitage, and then the frost came and spoiled things apparently. But, even with such handicaps, the practical result itself was most convincing of the value of a garden.

RECORD OF A GARDEN—SIZE 64 x 134 FEET

Asparagus	$7.80
Lettuce, curly and head	4.17
Spinach	4.50
Strawberries	6.38
Currants	.96
Gooseberries	1.82
Peas	8.13
Beets	2.50
Summer squash	.65
Winter squash	.75
Corn	3.60
Melons	.50
Cauliflower	.90
Seed potatoes	.50

Carrots 6.40
Tomatoes, ripe 7.80
Tomatoes, green 2.50
Beans, snap 15.00
Beans, kidney shelled .... .60
Lima beans 9.60
Okra .... .15

Total $85.21

Every summer offers to country women better opportunities for successful gardening than ever before. Each year more and better instruction in every phase of gardening and in the use of garden products is given absolutely free by the department of agriculture at Washington and by the state colleges. Plants and seeds from Washington are sent free. . In New York state, we may study gardening in Cornell Reading-Clubs. In all parts of the state, canning and community clubs have been organized where every one receives, free, all sorts of instruction pertaining to the home; where scientific instruction is given in fruit and vegetable canning, in order that every bit of surplus fruit and garden products may be utilized to the best possible advantage. Similar privileges are available in other states.

The tremendous need of conservation along these lines because of the scarcity of food during the war made very apparent the excellent work done by the state colleges in the way of organization and instruction, in the country districts especially. Great waste of food products had for years been necessarily going on in the country away from markets and out of knowledge of the big needs of town and city. The war brought the women of city and country together in a new bond of common sympathy, in a new knowledge of human needs. In the new years coming, country women will be ready to meet the city's need in a sympathetic, intelligent, generous way. The great thing for the farmers' wives and daughters to do, as never before, now that we see so clearly beyond the measure of our own needs, our own larder, beyond to our world-neighbors' empty shelves,—is to go ahead and make gardens.

Every country woman, in the older states at least, is bound sooner or later to become a gardener. Let us all do it this very summer. Let us make up our minds to raise all our own vegetables and more than we need, enough for our own use during the entire season and some over of the best for our city neighbor; enough, also, for canning for winter use for our own larder and plenty to help fill the empty shelves of our world neighbors. Then let us, every one, make up our minds to eat more vegetables and, in that most satisfactory way, cut down our meat bills and

grocery bills and doctor bills, while as a natural
consequence we grow more independent, richer,
healthier, happier. Thus even against odds, perhaps even because of odds, may we have gardens.

III

ESTABLISHING THE NEW GARDEN

HAVING settled the question of entering the realm of gardening with all its high adventure and sure returns on investment, the next thing is when to begin. Any time is the time. March, perhaps, with most astonishing weather for that most uncertain month; country roads blocked and big drifts piled to the eaves of the barn; with the wind sweeping over the gardens buried deep; and the snow still coming down. Midwinter weather in March may mean that spring is well on its way. We may be sowing garden seeds soon. It is time anyhow to be making our plans. So let us be at it and at least decide on a place for our garden.

The location is most important. Choose a permanent place, if possible. It is unfortunate to be obliged to move the garden. No penny-wise advantages of moving a garden once established can outweigh the disadvantages. Changing a garden may, in some ways, be good for crops; but it is not so good for the gardener. It somehow blurs the memories. Choose the location for life, if possible. Keep it, if you can manage,

13

where first you began to grow something, where first the vision came. It should, of course, be convenient to the house; but it is of greater importance that it be out of sight and sound of the house. Perhaps a grove or an orchard or, maybe, only a group of trees intervenes between the house and the best available garden site; but it must be secluded in some way. There should be shrubbery and shade trees nearby where birds are likely to nest. Beneath one tree, there must be a seat in full view of "the hills whence cometh our strength" or in sight of a wood with its quiet depths and perhaps the cool sound of a brook somewhere. Such a situation would make the out-door home ideal. Anyway, if the worker is to get all possible good from the garden, she must feel, once there, that another world surrounds her, with other thoughts and other interests. She must feel free to enjoy her out-door home.

The size does not matter much. Begin with a smaller garden than you aspire to own some day. Force yourself thus to make the most of what you do own. A neglected garden is a pitiful thing. One feels almost human sympathy for the half-starved misused plants. Keep the size of your garden well within the measure of your time and strength, for then it will always furnish refreshment and recreation.

Having found the right place and put a limit to the size, we will hope to find the soil suitable.

A deep sandy loam, well drained, is the very best garden soil. The sand seems to hold the heat and so warms the entire soil; and in that way, early growth is assured. The particles of sand prevent packing and make room for air. A loam is naturally fuller of plant fiber than are other soils, and, therefore, retains moisture well. If it is kept full of humus, that is, of decaying animal and vegetable matter, it will be loose and crumbly, friable, and will not bake. If below the sandy loam there is a gravelly layer, the garden will have excellent drainage. This constitutes ideal soil.

Some kinds of soil may be easily improved, almost made over. To the soil which has too much sand or gravel, we will add, when the garden is prepared, all the vegetable fiber we can get:— well-rotted horse manure, material from the compost heap, litter from the hen-house, rakings from the lawn, and leaves—anything that will give it body. To succeed at all with clayey soil for general gardening, stuff it with humus; but avoid clay soil, if possible, however enchanting the surroundings.

The general preparation must be careful and thorough. The fall is really the time to start the new garden. The plowing comes first. Fall plowing makes it possible to begin work much earlier in the spring and so saves the gardener's time when it is most precious. It also improves the physical character of the soil, especially with heavy loams or stiff clayey soils. Those that are sandy are usually more unvariable in texture and are open and ready to be worked at any season.

The compacted soils, however, need more careful attention. The freezing and thawing of the cold-weather months and the action of the snow break up the lumps of clay and lighten the heavy loam. The plowing should be done as soon as the land begins to moisten through the early fall rains. The depth of breaking up a garden for general use depends on the kind of soil, largely. Hard soils need deep plowing. Sandy soils, especially those so full of gravel at the bottom that they tend to leach, should be worked nearer the surface, thus allowing the lower layer to become more compact. Sod land should be turned over well above the frost line for the sake of the action of the freezing not only on the texture, but also in disposing of all life that may prove a menace to plant growth. The depth should vary with different seasons, also, on the same kind of soil, making a kind of rotation in plowing. This practice improves the physical make-up, producing a more even texture as regards depth; and it also conserves plant-food; and, with most soils, improves the drainage. The subsoil needs, occasionally, to be broken up and brought nearer the surface, in order that we may get the best possible value from the land. For that purpose a subsoil plow may be used if the farm possesses one. Otherwise merely plow very deep. One variation of the ordinary kind of plowing is of especial value with a poorly drained soil and with one so placed that it dries out too slowly in the spring. Plowing called "ridging" assists greatly in surface drainage; and the ridges lying up and open to the sun and to the action of the air through them are thus ready for use much earlier. Such careful discriminating preparation of the ground accomplishes much towards the making of a really successful garden.

The fertilizing comes next. Much of the plant-food for the season's growth needs time to make it ready for use. The complete disintegration of the material and the necessary chemical action will take place during the late fall and winter season. Therefore, autumn is the time to provide the main supply of food. By fertilizers are meant here all manures and composts and other natural materials in which the fertile or food-producing substances are partly ready for use. These natural fertilizers do not include the quickly available commercial products. The very fact that this plant-food is quickly available, ready for use, assumes that unless immediately utilized it may waste. For that reason, commercial fertilizers are not applied until near seed time. For the fall cover, use only well-rotted manures or other thoroughly decomposed fertilizers; or, best of all,

a generous supply from the oldest available compost heap. This avoids introducing into the new
garden a variety of pests like May beetles and
other forms of animal life injurious to plants.
With this thoroughly decomposed material, use
air-slaked lime, especially if the piece is sod land.
Spread it all over the surface. Plowed under,
such plant-food would be wasted below the level
of the average plant growth, carried off in the
drainage. Spread evenly on top and go over the
garden once with a drag. Now our new garden
is all ready for winter.

IV

PREPARATION OF THE OLD GARDEN

FOR the garden already established, even more attention is needed. The refuse must first be disposed of. When possible, this should be done during the season as each special crop is used. In the fall, after the crops are entirely harvested, a bonfire should be made of the refuse. Everything should be burned that may be diseased or harbor pests, and also all growth too heavy and coarse to be plowed under for humus. This will destroy garden pests and plagues and also save fertilizer, for the burned refuse is especially rich in potash. The garden crops harvested and the ground cleared, we are ready to plow; or nearly ready, for, if the time and extra work can be spared, a good measure of salt and lime spread over the garden will be a great improvement, an addition to our investment, both in the new garden and in the one already established. The older the garden, the more it needs the salt and the lime. The lime will sweeten the old sour soil; it is especially good for clayey soils, breaking up, slacking the hard clods; the salt will enliven and enrich all soils; and both will act also as fer-

tilizers and will do much to rid the garden of
insects. Spread on the salt and lime thick
enough to whiten the surface, and drag it in.
Let it lie a few days and drag again. It will be
wise to wait now until a good heavy frost
has made a finish of the troublesome live things.
Then, when the soil is moist, plow and fertilize
and drag again. Use the same procedure in plowing and the same care in choice and application
of fertilizers that was followed in establishing the
garden; and year after year, the old garden will
become a better investment, yielding richer returns.

At the close of the year something may be done
to carry out our theories on garden improvement.
We will consider first the texture of the soil.
If it is too light, not loamy enough; or if, on the
other hand, it is too compact, hard like clay, it
needs humus; and autumn is the best time to
furnish this valuable constituent. Humus improves the water-holding capacity of sandy soil
and lessens disastrous effects of drought. Plow
under all the humus-providing material that is
obtainable. The uninfested and undiseased garden refuse may be used. It is possible to cultivate
the late garden too clean. Let the weeds remain
unless they are going to seed. Scatter clover as
soon as each crop is removed, especially on clay or
very heavy loam. A clover crop turned in makes
humus and also furnishes green-manure. Before

plowing, add leaves and rakings, strawy manure, and old bedding and litter from the hen-house. Put everything of this sort well beneath the surface. All manures and vegetable fibers not entirely decomposed should always be put under by deep plowing. There, away from the surface and the loss through evaporation, chemical action may produce plant-food without waste.

Autumn is a good time to look out for better drainage. Naturally drained soil is, of course, most satisfactory. However, much can be done through artificial means to improve the condition in this respect. All open ditches should be kept clear, free from growth or anything that would hinder the rapid flow of the water. Ridging also aids in improving texture by disposing of surface water. These means, however, are only temporary. Permanent under-surface drainage is better and more lasting and accomplishes much in improving the soil texture. Stone ditches, if placed a good distance beneath the surface, do fairly well in carrying off the surplus water, unless the dirt clogs among the stones. These break down, however well built, after a time. The best and most permanent drains are those constructed of tile. They cost more at the start, but they last much longer and are far more satisfactory. The deeper the tiles are laid, comparatively speaking, the better will be the results. Place them from 3 to 4 feet deep, and near enough to dispose of the standing water. The result will be a great improvement in texture. The water settling in the soil renders it impenetrable, hard, impervious. Removing the superfluous water lightens the soil, makes it more open, porous, friable. Through capillary attraction, more water can then be held in readiness for the roots; and they can more easily make their way into the lower soil. Good drainage means also the utilization of plant-food. As the roots reach down deep, feeding on the newly unlocked food as they go, they grow long and straight and big and tender. Good drainage means using all the garden from top to bottom, making use of the entire store of food. That means producing bigger crops of crisp better-flavored vegetables.

Much can be done in the fall to make the garden tidy for winter. A large part of the pruning may be performed then, for as a rule pruning should follow fruitage. All seeds may then be sorted and stored in a dry place. The equipment ought to be looked over as it is removed and put away safe from damage. Wire netting, bean poles, stakes, and boxes should be piled under cover. Water pipes must be drained and put up out of the reach of the frost. Fences should be mended; garden seats repaired; and all things put in order.

When spring comes, it will need to be decided whether it is best to plow again. A disc harrow might do better. The layers of soil may be about where we want them. Plowing twice every year, unless the depth is much varied, brings to the surface, each spring, nearly the same soil for a seed-bed; and that would not be frugal gardening. On the other hand, shallow plowing may be an advantage. It will lighten, aërate a heavy soil; by that means, surface drainage will be improved; and the soil will become dry and warm and ready for planting much sooner. The best time for re-plowing is when the ground has warmed and dried enough to crumble easily. If it is plowed while still wet, the soil will be lumpy all summer. Give the lumps here and there a kick with your toe. If they fall to pieces readily, then you may expect the heavy soil below to be suitable for breaking up. Plow it shallow, always, when re-plowing. Dragging is all that will be necessary in the spring for a sandy soil. We must next put on whatever additional general fertilizer we intend to use. In the fall, we plowed under in the new garden material that needed time for disintegration and chemical action before being ready for use as a plant-food. Now, in the spring, we will leave near the surface a quickly available fertilizer.

Do not use much, if any, barn manure in the spring; use a good commercial fertilizer. The garden books and bulletins will explain in full detail what kind of fertilizer is best and how much to use. We must furnish the three most necessary constituents for plant development and those most often lacking: nitrogen for vigor, phosphorus and potash for good results. A complete fertilizer, one good for potatoes, will answer at first very well. It contains all three of these necessary foods in a proportion ready to feed the average plant well. The biggest part of the bulk is made up of a filler, a material used to save waste in handling and storing and to make it possible to distribute the chemicals evenly. When large quantities are needed, or when one kind of plant-food is to be used for a special purpose, the chemicals should be bought separately and mixed as needed. Spread it broadcast, evenly, thickly enough to show a little gray on the surface. Now comes the dragging, the finishing. For that purpose, any farm tool useful in the preparation of the cabbage field is satisfactory. The drag, the harrow, any fine horse tool will do. Drag lightly but thoroughly. In the best way possible, with the best tools accessible, the work must be continued until the soil is as fine and loose, as mixed and mellow as it can be made. Now, at length, our much-hoped-for garden is ready for planting, waiting for the seeds.

Perhaps now, after all that has been said concerning the important matter of getting a garden ready, the little back-yard garden plot may seem to have been forgotten. That is far from true, however. Size does not matter, you know. There may be just as much variety and adventure, just as much rest and inspiration and joy in the tiny garden behind the town or city home as in the wide spaces of a country garden. There is certainly less danger of fatigue and disappointment. Trees and bushes or vines make the needed seclusion; and the change from the hot city streets to the hidden shaded rest of the garden is peace itself. Of course, the plot is too small for teamwork; and, instead of a plow, you must use a spade and a hoe. But spading is the very best way to prepare a garden; and the more of your labor, yourself, you put into a garden, the more the garden is yours.

V

LAYING OUT THE GARDEN

In the laying out of the garden, whatever the size may be, there is more than one thing to be taken into account. Naturally we will consider personal choice as to what shall be grown. In addition, beauty and convenience of arrangement are to be considered; the location of different sorts of plants with reference to ease of care and their best growth; and, ever and always, the proper attention to the garden, with the future in mind.

Let us decide first what to grow in the permanent part of the garden,—the perennial garden. We cannot get on without the small-fruits. We will decide to have at least a few plants of each kind. The raspberries and blackberries might be put on the orchard slope. They will have fine drainage there and, once started, will do well. Down nearer the garden might be grown the currants and gooseberries, some grapes and strawberries. There will be keen enjoyment in growing them, and small-fruits grown properly will yield a nice little income and more. We cannot afford to miss the fun of growing our big brown gooseberries; of looking for the largest stems of cur-

26

rants hidden away among the leaves and finding, in the most sheltered clump of branches, a chippy's nest with its four speckled eggs and, down below, the little brown bird herself, half trusting and half afraid. That find pays for all the care the currants need for a year; and the currants will grow much better and there will be more of them because of the tiny home the bush shelters. Well earned is house and the fruit they eat, by the lice and the worms they destroy. When the currant jelly is placed on the Thanksgiving dinner table, we will think of the little brown bird; and the jelly itself will be richer in color, more tender in texture and fresher in flavor, because from beginning to end we made it ourselves.

In the summer time, when the unexpected or much invited guest comes to the breakfast table, if we may offer a cluster of fresh ripe grapes with the bloom untouched, the memory of the country breakfast will be lasting in pleasure. If we may offer a piled-up plate of strawberries for supper, our guest will never leave us willingly, —at any rate, not while the strawberries keep ripening. If the right kinds are grown, strawberries will continue ripening until long after frost in the very late fall. All of these small-fruits are sure to grow well, if properly cared for, and are certain to bear plenty of luscious fruit.

There are two more perennials that we cannot afford to leave out of the permanent garden. Pie-plant or rhubarb given a place with the other carefully tended plants is far different from the old uncared-for clumps starving in a neglected burdock corner. This old-timer repays every bit of extra attention with surprising returns. Along a garden walk (Plate III) or by the side of the fence or among the perennials, the rhubarb may be placed; but do not neglect it.

Asparagus has come to be indispensable in the home garden and is better grown and more appreciated each year. The asparagus beds come into bearing at the time when we are hungry for green things in the spring; and, in the long winters, the canned asparagus may be always at hand.

The arrangement of the garden, as regards the annual vegetables, is an illustration of conservation. There are many skillfully prepared plans suited to all kinds and sizes of gardens. It will be necessary, in large measure, at first to follow a plan, while gradually coming to understand the principles on which they are based. The laying out of the garden will be somewhat a matter of convenience. The rows will of course be parallel. They should run as nearly as may be north and south. That will insure sunshine among the plants, whenever there is sunshine anywhere. In that way, also, certain plants may serve as shelter for others. Those injured by too

II.—Farm Home and Garden.—A place in the open country.

much sunshine may be grown on the shady side of tall plants. For convenience in special fertilizing and cultivating, it is an advantage to grow related plants near each other. Parsnips and salsify are usually grown in rows by themselves. They need about the same kind of land and require nearly the same cultivation and both must have an entire season for development, even being left in the ground over winter to perfect the texture and flavor. Place them by themselves and out of the way of the fall plowing. Perhaps all the "roots" could be grown in a plot by themselves. Nearly all varieties of greens and salad plants should be grown in a separate group of rows. By this sort of arrangement of related vegetables, convenience and eccnomy of labor may easily be secured.

The question of garden conservation, however, is far more than merely a matter of convenience. We should plan to carry out some form of crop rotation. By that means we secure the best crops, both as to quantity and also quality; the soil receives more uniform cultivation; and plant-food is kept most evenly balanced. Crop and soil rotation have long been considered essential to good farming. It is even more necessary in a garden that is to be permanent. We will assume that the careful preparation of the garden has made the soil as nearly evenly balanced as possible; that is, so far as the main plant-foods, potash, phosphorus and nitrogen, are concerned. For that reason, we may grow whatever convenience indicates, on a particular plat, the first year. One season will give us the pulse of the garden as regards fertility in general and, also, the balance of plant-food. After that, in our planning we must take into consideration economy and best use of plant-food.

In considering garden conservation from this point of view, we will suppose, taking the simplest illustration in mind, that, after the first crop, a particular plot has an over-supply of nitrogen. All plants are fond of nitrogen. Some need large amounts; others are injured by over-eating nitrogen. If peas and beans are grown on soil that has too much nitrogen, they are certain to satisfy their voracious appetite for this food. Nitrogen makes vine and foliage especially. That is unfortunate in this case, for the greedy peas will run to vines. Certainly legumes must not be grown on that particular plat. Corn is also nitrogen-hungry, but it will use without injury, as it needs a large amount to grow well. The corn will thrive on the piece that has an over-balance of nitrogen. The nitrogen will make vigorous leaf growth. The phosphoric acid and the potash will be ready to make the ears. The fact that the corn will be making its greatest development during the warmest weather is an added advantage. Warm weather is the time when the organic forms of nitrogen furnished the garden through the humus in fall preparation are becoming most rapidly available for plant-food. The corn, thus given an abundant and constant supply of nitrogen, will make continuous luxuriant growth. We shall have many big succulent ears as a result; and the extra nitrogen will thus be disposed of. After the corn, this particular plat is ready the next season for the legumes. The peas and beans then will not grow merely vine and leaves. Plenty of pods will develop rapidly; and we may expect a big early crop of crisp beans and delicious tender peas.

The most interesting fact concerning these leguminous plants is their ability to make a part of their own food and, also, to provide nutriment for other plants. You have heard it said that bean-growing is good for a run-down abandoned farm. Corn has a different relation to fertility and it exhausts the food supply to a large degree and seems to make no returns. The legumes, however, not only take nitrogen from the air and the soil for their own provision, but they render this food available for other plants as well. You will easily find their little food factories after the peas and beans have begun to grow well. Pull up a bunch of beans, and there on the roots you will see the tiny nitrogen factories, the nodules. Some of the nitrogen is left in the soil.

The plant-food balance, however, may be again destroyed. There may be an over-supply of nitrogen, and a decrease in potash and phosphorus. To even things up, we must grow on that plat again some vegetable that needs a large quantity of this leaf-producing food and can thrive on comparatively small amounts of potash and phosphorus. Salad plants and greens are precisely the right choice. The more nitrogen foliage plants can get, the faster they will grow and the bigger and tenderer and richer colored will the leaves become. These foliage plants will make lusty growth, and the balance of plant-food will again, supposedly, be secured. Growing these vegetables having different kinds of root growth has, as well, brought about a more uniform cultivation of the soil. A three-year rotation in both crops and soil has consequently been carried out.

One or two general conclusions may be drawn and suggestions therefrom given. Always follow legumes with foliage plants or those making big growth of vine. Use plants needing little potash and phosphorus where those have been grown which tend to exhaust the soil of these elements. While these suggestions are especially intended for use in making rotation by seasons, they may easily be put into practice during one year. Successive cropping is merely a short rotation. When late spinach or celery or lettuce is grown after early peas, this plan is followed. Grow brussels

sprouts and cauliflower after the first beans.
Careful trials should be continued. By such a
procedure, many more things than one are accomplished. A uniform cultivation is secured and
the soil texture kept in the best condition; a more
even balance of plant-food constituents is maintained and, by it, the best economy practiced; and,
all the while, more and better vegetables are
grown and, perhaps without realizing it, the gardeners themselves are growing richer in more
ways than merely in vegetable possessions.

VI

TOOLS AND SUPPLIES

NEEDLESS to say, tools and garden supplies will
be essential to success but not such a variety of
tools, however, as one might at first decide. A
tool just right for the particular piece of work is
the one to choose; the one that will perform the
largest number of different kinds of work most
easily and quickly and in the best manner is the
tool to own. A hoe has always been considered
as indispensable almost as the garden itself. In
the old days, farmers always hoed the garden;
nothing else seemed to be needed. With due respect to old times and old gardens, it is to be said,
however, that a hoe is the very worst of all tools
unless used correctly. It is needed in hilling and
it is fairly useful in cutting weeds, when they get
such a start that cultivating does not dispose of
them. Even then, hoeing should be followed
straightway by surface tillage to prevent waste of
moisture. There is no other use for an ordinary
hoe. A little old bent hoe has been my useful as-
sistant for four busy years and is still better than
new, in some ways. Its light weight and bent blade
make it perfect for use among small plants. The

blade bent toward the row easily draws the soil close to the delicate seedlings, and makes it possible to keep the soil over the young roots without injuring the tops. At the same time, its filed edge snips off any weeds starting along the row. After the rows of seedlings are thinned, the small blade is able to work close around each plant. Such a hoe is as useful as a small hand-weeder, with the added advantage that the long handle enables the worker to avoid the strain of constant bending.

The best all-around garden implement is the potato hook. Select it yourself; see that it is light in weight; that it hangs right, is properly balanced. Out-doors, as well as in-doors, ease of work depends much on the tool. A potato hook is worth far more than a wheel cultivator. With it, the rows may be deeply and evenly prepared for seeding and ridged up, as well, when desired; the stones, all but the very finest, whipped out of the way. Then, turned over, the bend next the handle marks the tiny furrow for the seed, while the back of the hook smooths the surface. Covering the seeds is managed perhaps more easily with the hoe, but a shove with the back of the hook will do it nicely and without the bother of changing tools. There is no better cultivator. With it, one may vary the depth to be cultivated, largely by the height at which the handle is held. No other implement works so satisfactorily along rows of roots, rendering the texture of the soil

even and fine for smooth, straight, unbranched
root growth. A rake aids in finishing the surface
for the finest seeds, but it scarcely earns its purchase otherwise.

The ten-cent store will also assist in furnishing
utensils; a small shovel, a pair of shears, a long-
handled metal fork, a trowel, a tablespoon, and a
tin cup. In addition to these, procure a short-
handled pointed shovel or a spading fork, a
sprinkling can, and two pails, a small one for
distributing extra fertilizer and a larger one for
carrying water. With these, the supply of tools
is complete enough.

All garden supplies must be ready at planting
time. Seeds should be selected early, varieties
chosen with care, amounts decided on, and the
order sent to a reliable seed house long before they
will be needed. That will insure the best seeds
possible. Sometimes seeds of the best varieties
and the highest quality may be entirely sold even
before March opens. Early purchase will also
allow time for testing germination. Look out for
all other supplies while there is time. Save all the
soot from every smoke pipe on the place. Store it
where it is dry. That will prevent waste, and it
can then be found, also, when needed. Have ready
a quantity of tobacco refuse. Tobacco dust or
scrap is as valuable in the care of the seeds and
plants as the potato hook is in the care of the garden. Sweepings may often be obtained at cigar

factories free, if an arrangement is made to be there on clean-up day. Do not get out of white hellebore, slugshot, and pyrethrum or fly-powder. They are a great aid in the fight to be waged against plant enemies. The probability is that, unless secured before beginning business, they will be lacking just when most needed. Get a ball of harvester's twine for a garden line. Buy two widths of fine-meshed chicken wire for training peas. Brushing peas is a nuisance; they do not grow so well on brush; some of the peas are wasted; and the disorderly rows injure the appearance of the garden. The wire is easy to put up and, with care, will last for several years; the peas do much better; and, grown in this way, are more convenient for picking and add much to the beauty of the garden. Manage to get cucumber and melon boxes, tomato supports and stakes for rows, and plenty of bean poles ready at odd times. All these supplies looked after and provided early will insure against delays when the garden season really opens.

Some thought must be given to the selection and provision of extra fertilizers. The commercial fertilizer used in the general preparation of the garden in the spring is, on the whole, the most satisfactory mixed fertilizer for the further work of starting and caring for crops. It is a 4-8-10 mixture, containing a proportion of 4 per cent nitrogen, 8 per cent phosphoric acid, and 10 per cent potash. If the amount of filler is small, it is termed high grade. Buy a bag of high grade 4-8-10 mixture and a few pounds of nitrate of soda and get some acid phosphate—the most readily available form of phosphorus. There should be plenty of wood-ashes and hen-manure on the farm. A garden might be run successfully on hen-manure or the sheep droppings and ashes. They are too valuable to be wasted.

All fertilizers should be protected from dampness. Nitrate of soda is an unstable compound and is modified rapidly in dampness. There is no fertilizer on the farm more valuable than hen-manure and sheep droppings and none so often wasted. When storing, throw over the droppings or fork in a little acid phosphate. Use as well a liberal sprinkling of land plaster or kainit (a cheap potash salt) on the dropping-boards after cleaning them. The plaster absorbs the liquid manure and so prevents waste of ammonia, which contains the nitrogen. Store the manure in tight and comparatively small receptacles; barrels will serve. The oldest and most thoroughly disintegrated fertilizer could thus be used first; and, also, there would be avoided a large waste which would be certain if the entire quantity were opened each time a little was needed. The ammonia odor is sufficiently convincing of the waste. Ammonia, like sodium nitrate, is volatile, and, as it evaporates, the nitrogen is lost.

For that reason, stoppers are kept in ammonia bottles, and air-tight covers should be kept on the supply of hen-manure. Covers can be dispensed with if acid phosphate is used with hen-manure. It retains the ammonia in a non-volatile form. Care in collecting and storing these especially valuable fertilizers will greatly add to their value and increase largely the garden income.

VII

PLANTING THE GARDEN

Do not plant too early. While the ground is becoming warm and dry enough, lettuce and radishes and onions may be grown in the hotbed. This satisfactory garden adjunct is always used for starting certain tender plants and those that require a longer season than the open ground would allow. Planting in the garden may be deferred until fairly warm weather has come, when the soil crumbles easily and, beneath the surface, it is not cold to the touch. Beware our cold springs and treacherous late frosts. If the gardener is in a great hurry, seed may be sown on rows ridged up high enough to allow the sunshine and warm air of mid-day to penetrate the soil. The earliest seeding should nearly always be made on ridged rows. By that means, a few rather tender varieties may be started sooner, if sufficient protection can be furnished for cold windy days and colder nights. The long-season sturdy vegetables, like parsnips and salsify, may go in as soon as the soil is prepared, without much regard to temperature. However, as a rule, early planting takes quite a risk of entire failure; and

40

almost always, at the best, sacrifices flavor and
tenderness even though the vegetables survive the
cold and frost and finally come to maturity. Even
the sturdy root vegetables, when started too soon,
make growth more slowly as a natural result, and
for that reason are fibrous and stringy and tough
and flavorless. Experience has proved that even
the hardy frost-resisting peas are often put in too
soon. Later peas have more than once matured
earlier than those planted two weeks before, while
the ground was still cold. The later peas made
continuously rapid growth and, for that very reason, produced more pods and tenderer peas and
were ready for the table much quicker. Steady
rapid growth is indispensable for the production
of large crops of tender full-flavored vegetables.

In planting, protection of the seed hastens
germination. Specific directions may be given
concerning distances between rows, amounts of
seed to be used, and depths of sowing and covering
for different varieties of seed. With a fair chance
and not too many hindrances, good seeds are sure
to grow. Seven lima beans may be expected to
produce seven sturdy lima bean plants. To bring
about this ideal condition, however, the seeds
must be safeguarded at the very outset against all
foes. · In spite of the care taken in its preparation to keep the soil free from invasion by garden
enemies, plenty of cutworm, wireworm and May-
beetle grubs are likely to be on hand, waiting until

moisture has softened the outer covering of the
seed. Then even before the germ has started to
grow, unless a protection of some sort is furnished
the seeds, the pests will eat their way into the
embryo and destroy the life. Either a deterrent
or a poison must be used. The latter requires
more special knowledge, and many kinds of seeds
might be thus injured; and there is always danger
in handling poisons. Tobacco dust is the best
deterrent. Sprinkle the dust or fine scrap thickly
in the row beneath the seeds, and nothing will
disturb them. The tobacco will not only be a protection to seeds during germination and early
growth, but later will furnish food.

For rapid germination, moisture and warmth
are necessary first; then stimulating food. To
start growth quickly, certain seeds may be soaked
in warm water until the outer shell is softened.
Seeds like parsley need long soaking. Peas and
beans make a much quicker start if their hard
cover is thus softened. All vine seeds, cucumber
and winter squash especially, should be first
sprouted on trays of warm earth or on a sod.
These various ways of hastening embryo growth
are a great assistance; but the best all-around aid
to germination is a heat-supplying stimulating fertilizer, one in which chemical action is still going
on, and, also, one which contains an unstable
nitrogen compound ready, in the presence of
moisture, to give up its nitrogen to stimulate the

growth of the germ. A big spoonful of the potato fertilizer at the bottom of the hill or beneath the row will furnish some heat, and its nitrate of soda will readily give up the nitrogen as a tonic for the embryonic plant. Better than commercial fertilizer for this purpose, however, is sheep droppings or the carefully stored hen-manure. A shovelful from the oldest barrel will make a tiny hotbed of each hill; and a sprinkle along the row will provide both the heat and stimulus so much needed. This plan of hurrying growth is particularly satisfactory in starting vines, anything that makes much growth before fruitage. It aids lima beans and okra and other warm-climate vegetables in adapting themselves to a shortened season. Whichever is used, care must be taken to cover the fertilizer with plenty of soil, lest the seeds should be burned. By this means will be furnished the heat so essential to rapid germination, and the stimulant so much needed for the tiny rootlets, the minute they start growing.

With plenty of warmth and a stimulant at hand to start growth, there must also be provided a sufficient and continuous supply of moisture. Soaking seeds is not enough. They would straightway dry out and be more impenetrable than before, unless a constant store of water were furnished. The necessary dampness is supplied by compacting the soil as the seeds are covered. This process of firming brings the particles of soil into close

contact with each other and with the seeds. A
regular little bucket line is thus formed, and the
water from the lower soil is passed along to the
seeds. Whether soil is firmed or not makes a
difference of several days in germination, especially in dry clear weather. Do more than give
the hill a pat with the hoe. Step on it or walk
straight down the row with even pressure. Sometimes, after compacting, the surface soil may begin to bake, as the dry heat or the cool breeze
passes over, contracting the surface. Tiny fissures
then appear, sometimes even before the seeds start.
This same bucket line, only another name for
capillary attraction, which furnished the water to
the seeds, is sending it on, past the seeds, through
the surface layer into the clear air. The moisture
is now evaporating. There is no danger of this
difficulty in damp heavy weather; but look out
when the air is drier and clearer than the soil, or
when there is a cold breeze, or after a heavy
pounding shower. As the surface bakes and
cracks, the seeds dry out and much of our care
and labor are for naught. Go along the row and
gently tap the soil or just barely scratch the surface with the hook or sprinkle on a little fine soil.
Toss a hoeful of the fine earth over the hills. The
dust mulch thus formed keeps the moisture where
it belongs, around the seed.

VIII

CARE OF THE GARDEN

FROM the germination of the first seeds until the harvesting of the last crop, there is always something to be done in the garden. However thorough the first work of soil preparation and seed planting, the final success depends on the attention that is given while the plants are growing. The proper care of the garden for the remainder of the season includes three things:—the best use of existing plant-food and moisture; intelligent increase of food and moisture; and adequate protection and care of growing plants.

The best use of the plant-food and moisture already in the soil at the beginning of growth is brought about by cultivation. The care of the garden used to mean weeding. It means that now only incidentally. Unless destroyed, weeds would be much more than an incident; but cultivation disposes of them before they have scarcely germinated. While including in its course destruction of those undesirable plants, the cultivator does far more. It brings the soil particles into contact with the fertilizer and both with the moisture, thus aiding chemical action. The more

45

the soil is mixed, the more actual use is made of the fertilizer present and the more readily moisture reaches the roots. To grow well, plants must have an abundance of food and water. Stirring the soil brings fresh food to the hungry plants; deep mixing and remixing brings the moist lower soil to the thirsty roots. Varying the depth of cultivation to fit the growth of roots secures the best results; shallower work for surface feeders, deeper tilling as the roots penetrate the soil. The fundamental thing is to till.

Tillage prevents waste of moisture. By frequent shallow stirring of the soil, a dust cover is kept on the garden. The soil particles in this mulch are separate. As firming brings the particles together and aids in securing water, so breaking up the surface crust separates them and keeps the water from evaporating. This theory put into practice during a drought often means saving the garden, making of it an oasis in the midst of parched fields. Such tilling is especially important early in the season, while the plants are making their greatest growth of foliage.

After large growth has been made and the roots have begun to feed deep, such frequent and careful surface cultivation is not so necessary. By that time, the heavy foliage covers or shades much of the surface and so prevents baking and cracking. Then, also, much of the moisture lost from the soil through evaporation returns as refreshing dew to the thirsty leaves. Until growth is well developed, however, whenever the soil begins to compact, go over the entire garden and stir the surface. Always cultivate after a shower. The harder the shower, the more the soil is pounded, the more it will bake and crack in drying. As soon as the water is absorbed and the soil is no longer sticky, cultivate. Do not wait until cracks appear. Go over every bit of the garden then, as soon as possible. Work backwards, drawing the potato hook toward you, back and forth, lightly and rapidly. Working backwards is the easiest quickest way and then no tracks are left to undo the work. In connection with this shallow surface tillage, any special cultivation may be done. The roots may need deep and careful work to loosen the lower soil and, getting rid of the stones, to make way for straight even growth. The corn may need hilling. Whatever is required in addition may be done; but always finish by stirring evenly the surface soil. The thrifty gardener intends to look out for waste. Then keep intact the dust mulch. Keep the cover on the garden by surface tillage.

The natural resources of the soil may be supplemented not only by conservation of moisture but, as we have already noted, by an increase of plant-food. Just as important as the stimulant to start growth is a wise use of extra fertilizers during the entire growing season. An intelligent addition to the food supply during the development of the vegetables makes the difference, in large measure, between an ordinary garden and gardening in scientific fashion. In the steady day-after-day care of the garden, we must still keep in mind that the correct amount of fertilizer applied at the right time is what produces prize-takers instead of ordinary vegetables. The knowledge of what fertilizer is best for different stages of development, how much to apply and when to apply it, requires study, experiment and experience. The science of feeding plants is necessarily inexact, especially because of the great variation in soils and the uncertainty as to the entire food content. To be sure of enough food, we must provide too much. At the same time, we know that too much of one fertilizer applied to certain plants makes rampant growth and little fruit. Equally true is it that too great a proportion of another will render the fruit coarse and fibrous and tough and flavorless. Lacking enough of a special kind of food, the fruit will not develop at all. We have to keep in mind the interdependence of plant-foods and observe development carefully, while we study this important and fascinating problem of the use of special fertilizers.

A little further and more concrete comparison of the special uses of these essentials to vegetable growth may be of value, just at this point in our study. We already know that plants growing foliage must have nitrogen; that phosphorus and potash are necessary to bring vegetables to maturity. It is equally true that, while the main function of nitrogen is to promote leaf growth, it is of great importance, also, in the production of quality of fruit. Phosphoric acid not only aids stalk and framework, but it hastens maturity and is essential in the perfection of the seed. Potash, the vegetable staff of life, packs the kernels of juicy corn as well as enriches the color of the tomato, and hardens the winter squash. Each, with its special function, is also essential during the entire season in supplementing some other form of plant-food. Throughout the whole process of development, from sprouting embryo to perfect fruit and seed, there must be an actual coöperation, a real working together on the part of these artisans of the garden.

Growth must have nitrogen. This constituent is found in every part of the plant. We used a fertilizer rich in nitrogen at seeding time. Equally valuable is a nitrogenous fertilizer for transplanting. The hen-manure and sheep-manure are also rich in immediately available nitrogen. Set the plants, as soon as they are removed from the hotbed, with a little of this manure below the roots. Take care that the fertilizer is well covered with soil, lest the tender roots be burned. Then, after a day or two, when the soil has settled, stir into the surface about the young plants a little more nitrate of soda. This compound contains the nitrogen in the form most readily absorbed and assimilated as food. Be careful not to allow it to touch the stems, and stir it well into the soil to save waste of nitrogen. Do this every few days. Use it in transplanting lettuce and celery. It is good for cauliflower and cabbage and brussels sprouts. With these foliage plants and with head varieties of lettuce, it may be used with advantage both in starting new growth after re-setting and, again, with another dose just as the heads begin to form. Follow the same plan with tomatoes and eggplant,—the heat-producing fertilizer below the roots when set, and the nitrate stirred in, at the surface, afterwards, until growth has well begun. All transplanting will be attended with much less delay in growth and with surer results, when this special kind of tonic food is provided.

After growth is well started, when a particular need of nitrogen is not indicated, use the 4-8-10. It may be relied on then to sustain healthy growth. There is sufficient nitrate in the mixture to provide for continued vigorous growth, as a rule; and it will insure big crops. It is sure to keep the potatoes growing well. Use a spoonful to a hill or a little along the rows, every few days, until the buds appear. There will be enough potash by that time to insure well-developed solid roots. Failure to supply potash when needed might result in famine in the potato hill. For lack of this food we may harvest only a few rough, ill sorted, misshapen potatoes, soggy and ill-flavored at best. After discontinuing the nitrate, for corn, this mixture is just right. The stalks will grow bigger and stronger; the roots will reach deeper; and the potash will aid in making a host of juicy golden ears. This combination is good for pole limas and for okra, after nitrate has well started the growth. Keep it up, a spoonful to a hill, every few days, until blossoming time. Then finish the season with wood-ashes. Use it, in the same way, with tomatoes and eggplant, and with all the vines except the salad cucumbers. With all vegetables except those grown for greens and salads, the procedure is generally, as follows: nitrate to start growth; 4-8-10 supplemented as needed to keep things going; and wood-ashes or some other form of potash to bring the harvest. This is, of course, heavy fertilizing and not all soils may need such liberal applications; the gardener must experiment with her own soil and carefully watch the results.

This coöperative plan of feeding will surely make the crops grow and it will accomplish even more. While this mixed fertilizer is furnishing all the food necessary to grow the biggest best crops, it may be at work in the soil. Ground limestone, ashes, and hydrated lime help decompose organic matter. They aid to break up the animal and vegetable matter, thus releasing plant-food, especially latent nitrogen. Big investments in food supplies bring bigger returns in crops and more still in additional food from the garden's miser hoard. This is particularly true when very early and choice results are to be obtained in a garden that is to provide home supplies.

To secure full advantage of extra fertilizing, both in the growth of crops and also in its power to make available inert soil food, the proper tillage must accompany its distribution. As we know well, these fertilizers are expensive, particularly the nitrate of soda. This valuable nitrogen container is liable to much waste. Being more soluble than other plant-foods, it is soonest dissolved and lost in the drainage unless immediately taken up by the roots. For that reason, only what seems needed is applied at one time. Cultivation should follow the distribution straightway. Also, any fertilizer is useless on the dust mulch. To be of any value, it must be brought into contact with the moist soil beneath the surface and placed where it can feed the roots. Therefore, as soon as a fertilizer is applied, cultivate. Make it a matter of convenience to do both pieces of work together, cultivating not merely to cover the fertilizer but to provide good growing conditions for the plant. Only good cultivators can make economical use of expensive fertilizers: these materials are not substitutes or makeshifts for tillage.

tilizer, but also for the general care of the plants.
If there is hilling to be done, hoe in the fertilizer
at the same time. Stir lightly for surface-feeding
roots; work in deeply for longer root systems. Increase the depth, of course, as the roots reach
down. By this plan of tilling when extra plant-
food is furnished will the most be made of these
special fertilizers in adding to the resources of the
garden.

The natural soil-moisture may be supplemented
by watering the garden. A dry season presents
difficulties not readily overcome. The principles
of dry-farming can often be put into practice with
surprising and joyous success. Frequent and
careful cultivation saves the store of moisture
and makes the best use of the food supply. Care
in preventing too much unnecessary growth and
too big an effort at fruitage also does much to help
in making the very most of the garden's limited
moisture resources. The result proves in a satisfying way that dry gardening pays. A drought,
however, is a serious handicap in growing prize-
takers. Much may be done to offset the difficulties
of a drought, if an extra water supply can be
furnished during the driest part of the season.

Better than dry-farming alone is watering.
There is a right way and a wrong way, however, to
water a garden. The wrong method is worse than
useless; it is actually injurious. Cold water
turned on the plants forcibly through the hose, in

the middle of a hot day or at night, is like a cold driving rain. It is a shock to their vitality. It may check growth instead of hastening development. If cold water is to be used, it should be turned on very early in the morning, before the air has begun to grow warm. Even then, it must not be applied to the plants themselves. It must be turned on to the soil. That will do fairly well, except for delicate plants and when the weather is very hot. The best way, however, is to use water about as warm as the air surrounding the plants.

The ideal watering equipment for a garden is the overhead system, an arrangement of horizontal parallel pipes placed well above the reach of growth and out of the way of cultivation. With piping located in this way the water is partly warmed by the hot air and sunshine surrounding the pipes. Small spraying nozzles are placed at intervals near enough to make watering the entire garden easy. However, such a system costs a good deal. Another plan is simpler and would cost much less; and, although it would mean more hard work, it would surely be satisfactory in results. The water might be run to the garden from the water supply through pipes laid on the surface, and then stored in an open trough until warm. Then, whenever it is convenient, the watering may be done.

Watering a garden must be performed thoroughly. Better not undertake it at all unless there is time to do it thoroughly. Undertake only a part of the garden at one time, practicing dry gardening on the remainder, meanwhile, if necessary. Take sufficient time and use enough water to penetrate the damp lower soil. How much will be needed may be found out by digging down beside one plant. Notice, also, how the water settles on the surface after the ground is thoroughly soaked. However much water is needed, be sure to use enough. Turn it on slowly, close to the stem. A convenient utensil for this purpose is the garden sprinkling pot with the sprinkler removed. Make a hollow around the stem if necessary, to keep the water from running off. Soak the roots clear through to the damp layer below. Connecting the moist lower soil with the roots by this means will establish capillary attraction. In this way, the extra water furnished helps the plants in making a more continued use of soil-moisture. Done thoroughly, in this manner, it will not be necessary to water oftener, usually, than once a week. Sprinkle the foliage of the smaller plants to clear them of dust and refresh them. As soon as the water is entirely absorbed, stir the surface. Put into practice what we know about conserving moisture. Since warm water is used and tillage follows, watering may be undertaken at any time of day.

Certain plants suffer more than others from

lack of moisture. All when set must have extra water to start them off. Foliage plants, especially, suffer from need of water. Any salad plant, to be succulent, must have an abundant supply. With many vegetables, the fruit will not form; the blossoms will not even set; the buds will wither and fall in very dry weather. Unless extra water is furnished, when so badly needed, much of the early labor of the gardener is lost, and the harvest will be materially lessened. A time of drought may be safely passed, however, by increasing the natural supply of water.

IX

INSECT PESTS AND DISEASES

LET us, at this point, assume for our encouragement that everything possible has been done to make the garden prosper. Proper seeding in correctly prepared soil has resulted in large strong germination. Intelligent persevering use of every means for promoting healthy rapid growth has brought about unceasingly vigorous development. A big harvest is assured, if the garden continues to flourish. Danger threatens, however. Disease may attack the plants; insects may destroy what the gardener's skill and toil have thus far accomplished. Protection must be furnished the growing plants. The fight to be made against these garden enemies should increase the interest. The harvest shall be ours. We do not intend to be worsted by rust and mildew; by cutworms and cucumber beetles. Adequate means are ready to wage successful warfare.

Everything that has been done to promote healthy growth is, in its very nature, at the same time a hindrance to disease. Proper cultivation and rotation of crops have done much to ward off ill health. The garden and the border free

57

from weeds keeps away untold numbers of these stealthy disease carriers. Garden sanitation is the biggest means to garden health. After all that has been done directly and indirectly, however, to bring about healthy condition, yet maladies of some sort almost continually menace the garden. Plant disease may be combated most effectively through preventive measures. Mildew, rust, dry rot, and blight, all fungous diseases, may be more easily prevented than cured. Healthy plants may be kept so by spraying.

Bordeaux mixture is considered the best fungicide for general use on garden crops. This spraying material is a preparation of copper sulfate and lime, in water. The chief uses of the lime are to make the copper sulfate stick tightly to the leaves and to neutralize its caustic effect; that is, to prevent it from burning the leaves. Rather than to prepare a small quantity, it may be more satisfactory for inexperienced gardeners to purchase a reliable mixture and dilute it as needed. Open only a small quantity at a time, because it is liable to loss. Make the first application just before disease signs appear. The material adheres closely to the foliage and, in dry weather, will remain for a long time. In dry weather, also, there is the least possible injury to the foliage, while dampness increases the caustic effect. To be most efficacious, the wash must cover every part of the plant. This, however, can-

III.—Rhubarb by a Garden Walk.

not really be accomplished by one spraying. For
that reason, let two applications be made at first,
within a few days. Afterwards, the frequency of
spraying may depend on the condition of the vegetables. Once in two or three weeks is often enough
while the plants look healthy. Wherever this
covers and as long as it remains, it prevents the
development of the spores of fungi. We must not
flood the garden with bordeaux, however. There
is danger, in spite of the lime, of burning the
leaves. Keep in mind the natural hindrance to
growth from closed leaf pores. Nevertheless, its
continued application is indispensable. Rain may
wash off the spray. New growth keeps coming;
new shoots continually come into sight. We must
be ever on guard. At the appearance of a fresh
onslaught by our ambushed foes on new growth
or always after a rain, counter attacks by
the bordeaux should be made every few days to
guarantee safety. The best apparatus for this
work is a force sprayer. A garden sprinkler may
be used with fair success, however. During the
summer of 19—, this spray was applied once a
fortnight by means of an ordinary sprinkling pot.
Potatoes, tomatoes, hollyhocks, strawberries,
grapes, melons and squashes, okra, and beans
were thus treated. The result was satisfactory.

Although free from disease, our plants may
still have to fight for their lives, a losing fight
without help from the gardener. Beetles and

worms will gnaw their leaves; lice will suck their juices; cutworms and grubs will prey on stem and root. These enemies—one or another or all together—are certain to invade the garden and sometimes when least expected. They are sure to ruin the plants attacked unless, straightway, they are fought with intelligence and persistence.

Measures may be taken to drive them away. Tobacco never does any harm in the garden; it may be used liberally. Scattered beneath the seeds, the tobacco odor keeps the grubs away. Use tobacco refuse always when transplanting as well. It is as necessary to the young plant then as a heat-producing stimulant and plenty of moisture. Sprinkle it thickly in the soil close to the stems of cauliflower, cabbage, and tomato plants. Its proximity will free the cauliflower and cabbages of cutworms; the wireworms will leave the tomatoes. Use tobacco around the strawberry plants to rid them of the wireworms and white grubs. Dusted over the potatoes and the tomatoes and scattered above the rows of spinach and beets, it will drive away the flea-beetles that riddle the leaves; it will prevent the leaf-miner from spoiling both beet greens and spinach. Soot accomplishes the same results; but care is needed in its use, for too much will burn the leaves, especially in damp weather. Sprinkle just a little on the foliage and scatter more of the soot on the soil or stir it in near the endangered plants. Cutworms on the corn and squashes may sometimes be entirely disposed of by soot or tobacco. Scatter a handful about the hill of corn early and place a little in the soil around the squash plants. Cornmeal has been used as a deterrent for the pests that gnaw, as also has road dust. Salt acts as a repellent and as a poison in ridding the cabbages of worms and the lettuce, sometimes, of snails. Lime spread over the surface helps to dispose of injurious life in the soil. It tends to kill the unhatched eggs and the larvæ.

Cultivation alone is of real value against insects. Merely stirring the soil close to the squash stems carefully with the finger, now and then, will usually prevent trouble with cutworms. It will do the same for tomatoes and cauliflower. Many a cutworm and grub has never even hatched for lack of opportunity. A stiff water spray from the hose will clean the plants of aphids, especially the sluggish wingless forms that collect on the leaves of the limas and spoil the appearance of the lettuce and gorge themselves on the peas. Whipped off by the hard fine spray, they seem unable to get back. Stirring the soil beneath them makes a finish of their depredation by smothering. All these deterrent methods will be of value.

Whenever it can be done, the simple method of hand-picking is the surest and safest means of ridding the garden of injurious live things. Whip off the potato beetles and the bugs and the currant worms over a pan into which has been poured a little kerosene oil. Hand-picking or pinching is the only way to make a certain end of the beetles. Of course, the flea-beetle is the exception. No one ever could catch garden fleas. This method followed with asparagus beetles disposed of both species almost entirely in a few years. There should be no reason to expect further trouble with them, if there is no wild asparagus growing near, and if the neighbors' gardens do not harbor the pests. Hand-picking or pinching is almost certain to dispose of cucumber beetles and squash bugs just as permanently. These squash bugs are well-nigh invulnerable against any other means of extermination. Driven from the vines, they hide away and bide their time; the cucumber beetles feed elsewhere and seem to increase astonishingly. Cucumber beetles will thrive on corn and beans. Driven on, they will live and apparently flourish on grass and weeds and wait their opportunity. When the winter squashes are beginning to ripen, before the shell hardens, these beetles will swarm over them and gnaw the shells until they are actually honeycombed and the squashes are ruined. Better pinch them, if you can, and be done with them. If the suggestion is unpleasant, wear gloves. The first unpleasantness will be forgotten when big, perfect, hard-shelled squashes are harvested. This method will not prove so troublesome as might

seem at first thought. Twice a day, for a few
days, may actually make a finish of them straight
off for the season. Perhaps a second invasion
may occur. After another campaign of the same
thorough kind, however, nothing more is likely
to be seen of them, except, maybe, a few stragglers.
These cucumber beetles are creatures of fixed
habits. Very early in the morning look for them
around the stem, just below the surface. In the
middle of the day, you will find them underneath
the leaves, many of them on the cool ground. At
other times, they are not so easily caught. Have
it in mind, the first thing in the morning, and
pinch the intruders. Go over the plants again
at noon. You may need to enlist your neighbor's
interest in his own garden, if he lives near by.

After all that has been done, it may be necessary finally to use real poisons. Bordeaux mixture, used primarily as a fungicide, is also an
insecticide. Its copper sulfate is somewhat
poisonous, even in the weak dilution used. This
spray alone is effective in killing bugs and
worms, especially those that subsist on the foliage.
For those that suck the plant juices, and for
those with more resistance, a stronger poison
may be needed. Slug shot and pyrethrum powders
are only slightly poisonous. Hellebore is stronger
and so more effective. Dusted over the currant bushes and the gooseberries, any one of
these powders may be expected usually to dis-

pose of the worms left by the spray. While poison-
ing their victims, they evidently smother them
also, like all the deterrents. These mild poisons
should be effective with potato bugs and cucumber beetles, any left alive after the other measures
have been used. Kerosene emulsion is especially
destructive for lice and insects, like the squash
bug, that suck their food. This insecticide is
merely a dilution of kerosene with water as an
emulsion. Like other oils, it can be held in solution only by means of force pumping, stirring
and beating until the oil-drops are thus evenly
distributed in the water. Soap, when dissolved
in the mixture, aids in emulsifying the oil. This
is, naturally, less injurious than clear kerosene.
Sprayed over the infested plants, it is very effective. Paris green is the strongest poison. It is
sure death to whatever eats it, insect, worm, or
grub. We may add paris green or other arsenic
to our bordeaux mixture. The same spraying will
then fight disease and kill the live things. Use
the farm supply of this poison spray, when available. Otherwise buy the commercial preparation
called Pyrox. One spraying with this insecticide,
after all the other measures used, will surely end
the fight victoriously against all the enemies of
our garden.

The gardener will have live assistants. The
birds will be on hand, all the time, some of them.
The robins will snap up the grubs and the cut-

worms turned out to the surface. Chippies and goldfinches are greedy for insects and lice. Encourage them all with nest boxes and materials to build. They will settle in the garden for life, coming back, every spring, ready for work. The robins may eat a good deal of fruit; but, in the end, the balance will be much in their favor. It does not pay to kill the garden snakes. They are harmless and they live on what is injurious to the garden. The ladybug keeps at the plant-lice from morning till night and never is seen to "fly away home." The big friendly toads are on the job, all day long. Look out for them; you will learn their haunts easily. They are out in the open, when it is cool. When it is hot, you will come across them under the mulch or in a moist corner or under what seems to be a clod of earth, their snapping black eyes on the watch.

X

LOOKING TOWARD THE HARVEST

In gardening, survival of the fittest is the law. The crowded rows of seedlings are given a better chance by thinning out the weakest poorest plants. If use can be made of the extra plants for greens or salads or for transplanting, select the strongest biggest ones. Thin the rows of spinach and beets for the earliest garden greens. Pull some of the lettuce for salad, to make room for heads to form. Thin out the okra, the beans, any plants growing too close for best development. After danger from insects is past, only the strongest plants are left in the hills of squashes and melons and cucumbers. Only the sturdiest are left to bear the crop.

After growth is well started, the vines must be trained to keep them from running wild. The limas must be twisted about the poles to start them off on their climb. The peas must be turned toward the wire netting used to support them and the soil hilled against the row to hold them in place. The ground vines need to be trained to make the best use of the surface.

Plants must also be checked as well as guided in

66

growth. If plenty of fruit is to come, careful
preventive pruning must be done. The limas are
snipped when they reach the top of the poles, else
the big beans will not all mature. Strawberry
runners must be cut off close to the plant if we
want to grow berries. The squash vines are
nipped at the end after two or three squashes have
set, and some of the side shoots are stopped.
Toward fall, squashes too late to mature are cut
from the vine. All the vines are pruned with more
fruit-bearing in mind. The tomatoes are carefully staked and pruned to one stem. All of the
branches are supposed to be cut off with a bare
half inch of growth that prevents another branch
from starting. We keep the suckers pulled from
beside the growing corn. By this means of close
pruning, plant vigor is turned into fruit-making.
Perhaps we snip a few of the latest buds from the
stems of tomato blossoms. Fewer tomatoes to
each plant, fewer squashes to each vine, mean
bigger, sounder, better-flavored fruit. As the season advances and the crops develop, the slow-
growing and imperfect, the misshapen and gnarly
specimens are cut off and destroyed. As the harvest time approaches, one essential seems left for
the gardener to look out for,—plenty of fresh air
and sunshine for the growing vegetables and fruit
Fungous diseases lurk in the gloom. Overhanging
leaves that make too dense a shade must be cut
away. In cloudy weather, the big limas nearest

the ground beneath the leaves ripen slower than those farther up the pole, in the light. The grapes are sour and dull-colored, when shaded too thickly. The tomatoes will barely turn color in the dark. The dark green of the Warted Hubbard is a sickly yellow on the side next the ground. All through the garden, the light and sunshine are especially needed to sweeten and flavor and color the ripening fruit.

XI

ASPARAGUS

THE most important thing about growing asparagus is to grow it. Put the young roots into the ground, right side up; furnish food and water; and you can scarcely keep asparagus from growing.

I should put the asparagus alongside the garden, between the annual garden and the perennials,—the small-fruits and other plants that remain in the ground over winter. Planning thus, the regular garden care and cultivation will be shared by the asparagus. Placed by itself, it is likely to be forgotten and the weeds are bound to grow and the grass is sure to creep in. Its graceful feathery appearance adds much to the beauty of the garden in summer; and placed where it is most likely to be cared for, its value will be indefinitely increased.

The garden will be thoroughly plowed in the fall. Put in an extra quantity of well-rotted manure along the strip being prepared for the asparagus. Too much fertilizer can scarcely be used, provided it is really well-rotted; that is, so completely disintegrated, broken up, that no live things—May-beetlegrubs, wiremorms, or cut-worms—can find food or warmth. The more material of that sort that is worked into the soil, the looser and fuller of air and the richer will be the ground, the more the young roots will have to feed on, the farther they will reach out in all directions, and the sturdier they will become. Thus prepared, let the ground lie until spring.

As soon as the snow is gone and the frost is out and the earliest gardening can be done, have ready the young year-old asparagus roots. Get them, if possible, of a nearby market-gardener. You may, of course, start with seeds, but that means uncertainty as to variety and a year of unnecessary waiting; and two years are long enough to wait before beginning to enjoy the results of your labor. The delay caused by starting with year-old roots instead of old ones pays well. Old roots do not transplant well, and two years should be allowed anyway, in order to give the plants a chance to get their roots well anchored and sturdy enough for the shoots to be cut. A hundred roots may do at first.

Arrange the crowns right side up, being careful not to break the rootlets. Place them far enough apart to leave plenty of room for growth, 6 inches at least and 10 inches below the surface, anyway, because asparagus roots are bound to work towards the surface.

Do not let the bed dry out, and be sure to give

the weeds no chance to grow. Unless the season is exceedingly dry, proper cultivation will provide or save moisture and also take care of the weeds. The motion of the cultivator will in itself prevent the weed seeds from sprouting and so stealing the food belonging to our young asparagus plants; and, at the same time, the mulch thus formed will save the moisture. These simple directions are the guaranteed way for starting asparagus. You may be sure of results.

You will be patient; but there's the rub. The young slender shoots are so tempting; but their slenderness shows lack of sturdiness in the roots, a necessity for a bed that will really be permanent. Tops must be allowed to grow in order to produce big sturdy roots. These, in turn, will send up bigger and tenderer shoots every year. So just be patient. Do not begin to cut for two years. Hold fast to your resolution. Keep the bugs away. Cut and burn the brown tops in the fall and provide a heavy cover for winter. Then be patient.

Finally the long look ahead is over; the two years are up; and we begin to enjoy our reward. The usual spring care has been given and the big stalks begin to appear. Cut them, one by one, with a sharp knife, below the surface. Do not sacrifice two or three beneath the surface just to get the one in sight. Cut carefully and leave soil over the place where the stalk is cut. Sometimes a tiny stalk appears among the big ones. I should pull that, because probably a seed has started growing over the big root. It will only be in the way. Cut all that are ready to be used.

During the heaviest growth, there will probably be much more than can be used fresh. Do not allow any to be wasted. Store away in jars whatever is left over from each cutting. Just dip the stalks into boiling water, because blanching makes packing easier. Cut up the tougher ends and sterilize for soup. Pack the tender tips whole. Use the pressure canner if possible, for long boiling injures the texture. At Christmas time, Thanksgiving, any time, use the canned asparagus in the various ways in which you ate it fresh. The tips are very appetizing, served hot with a dressing of melted butter on crisp toast. Served cold with mayonnaise dressing, it is very good. The asparagus water makes a delicious cream soup stock—no one will guess it was "canned."

XII

BEANS

We need to know beans as seed first in order to succeed in growing them. A good plan is to grow your own seed. In that case, choose the earliest, largest, healthiest, cleanest looking specimens to provide the seed. Leave a group of sturdy plants for that purpose. Give them a little extra care in the way of cultivation. Feed them more phosphorus and potash. Do not disturb them by picking any of the fruit. That in itself will serve as a protection from disease. Now, from these special plants, when the beans are thoroughly ripened, select the pods that are free from disease, the troublesome rust, anthracnose. Next, when shelling, sort out and save only the fully developed, plump, biggest beans. Only completely ripened seeds will be productive, only plump seeds will have enough food stored in the cotyledons, the food-leaves, to make sure of a vigorous start. Finally these precious sureties of another harvest must be stored in a cool dry place.

All kinds of beans may be expected to mature early enough to provide seed, except the limas. For these, in central New York climate, we may go to the dealer. In depending on the market for seed, choose the most reliable dealer. Use varieties that have been tried out and found excellent, that have become standard. It does not pay to use "specialties," new varieties, unless just a few are tried for the pleasure of the experiment. It might be helpful to name some varieties that have been favorites. For limas, Early Leviathan pole limas are satisfactory. The bush limas may be grown, and they are somewhat earlier; but the flavor is not usually so fine, and they are much smaller and drier and the crop is not so large. The extra trouble in growing pole limas, in securing and placing the poles and training the young growth, is forgotten when the beans are harvested.

For "snap" beans that are never string beans, that break brittle and are plump and crisp, you must get the Golden Scimitar Wax, if possible. The crop has failed for a few years, and the Refugee Wax was substituted. That, also, is an excellent variety. The kind to look for, if you hunt the catalogue list, is the bean that is long and round and golden yellow and that breaks with a snap. That is my choice. Perhaps you prefer a green bean. It must have the same qualities, aside from the color. The salad bean should be green; it makes a more attractive salad, to my thinking. There are varieties offered,—a long, slender, tender bean of a fresh green color, just right for salad. Or any snap bean may be used for salad,

if gathered before the seed begins to form. For
all snap beans, the bush varieties are just as
good, even better than the pole sorts. Beans growing on the poles add to the attractiveness of the
garden, however. For a pole bean, the Old Homestead and the Speckled Cranberry are excellent.
The Old Homestead is the most popular green
snap bean. The Speckled Cranberry is especially
good as shell beans, like the limas. They are a
deep brown in color and have a rich flavor.

In planting beans, we need to have the soil in
proper condition and to know the right time and
the best method for putting in the seeds. Only
a word is necessary with reference to the soil;
that which has been prepared properly for general garden use is right for beans. Give the bean
strip careful cultivation just before planting.
The time is important. Beans are tender and cannot withstand the frost. For that reason, they
usually should not be put in until danger from
frost is over. The seeds decay quickly, when the
soil is cold and wet. So do not plant until the
ground is warm and dry, or just moist. A few
bush snap beans may be risked earlier, if they
are warmed by means of a heat-producing stimulant placed under the hills and protected by some
covering like melon boxes. If an untimely frost
threatens when the seedlings are just starting, a
cover of soil may be hoed over them. The frost
limit varies so much and settled weather is so

uncertain that it is necessary to have at hand means of protection. Therefore, the first full planting of snap beans should be in rows. The stakes with the garden line attached for marking may be left with the line about a foot above the row. Then when an unexpected cold night threatens, newspapers may be laid over the line. By this simple means, I have carried beans and other tender plants safely through a long cold spell. While it is well to have means at hand for protection against the frost and cold, it is best, as a rule, to delay planting until warm, dry, settled weather has really come. The tenderest varieties, like the pole limas, should wait until "ten days after corn planting time."

Now for the planting. Soaking the beans in warm water over night shortens the time necessary for germination. Make the furrows for the snap beans less than 2 inches deep. Even the big limas should not be covered more than 2 inches. Scatter tobacco dust beneath the seeds. Put a little hen-manure under the rows of the first planting of snap beans. Place the beans 3 or 4 inches apart and stem side down, if you want the fullest quickest germination. If the soil is very heavy, cover more lightly. Do not forget to firm the soil.

After the weather is certainly warm and settled, I like to put the plantings of bush beans in hills—big broad hills, 3 feet or more apart. Use a half dozen seeds to a hill, sowing far enough apart to let in the sunshine and to allow for full development of each plant. Plenty of light and sunshine among the plants is a good prevention of "rust." Arrange the hills alternately, in parallel rows. The result is very attractive when the big clumps of healthy plants begin growing; and this arrangement of growth brings about the best results in fruitage. A succession of bush beans may be grown. Plant a few every fortnight. When growing climbing beans, use the same big hills, and follow the same arrangement, only set the pole first and then plant the beans around the pole. For limas, follow the same plan as for snap pole beans, in the main. The lima hills should be farther apart, 4 feet being a good distance. With these big beans, special care is needed in placing them at an even distance around the pole and in setting them stem side down. These beans are very liable to rust and decay and are most delicate. For that reason, germination should be aided as much as possible. Sometimes, when the soil is heavy and hard, the tender seedlings are injured in attempting to break through the soil cover, especially when the beans are planted upside down. Their effort to turn over and release the cotyledons and reach the air breaks the tender seed-leaves often and, sometimes, the stem itself. Therefore, set the seeds with stem side down and cover lightly. Limas are especially liable to attacks from cutworms. For that reason plenty of tobacco should be scattered among the seeds. With care in planting good seed at the right time, a big start has been made toward an excellent harvest.

Not much more care is needed except, perhaps, a little extra food once or twice and regular cultivation. Some attention may need to be given the seeds before they start. If there should be a heavy pounding rain and the surface should harden and crack, then, as we already know, the surface mulch must be restored in some way. If the beans are beginning to start, dirt must be scattered over the hills and up and down the rows. There is more difficulty in that regard with beans than with almost any other seed. As soon as they start, a little extra nitrogenous food may be given the young beans in order to hurry up growth. One application of nitrate of soda may be given, a tablespoonful to a hill and a sprinkle along the row. That is enough on a rich loam. Perhaps one more application might be made, if the soil is poor. There is danger, however, of giving legumes too much nitrogen.

After the first few days, the main attention should be given to cultivation. Be especially careful not to cultivate when the plants are wet, when the dew is on the foliage or when it has rained. Even going among the plants, touching them when they are damp, tends to increase "rust." Culti-

vate when the sun is shining; and cultivate often.
When stirring the soil, watch out for signs of anthracnose. If it does begin to show, then use the
bordeaux mixture. Blight, a disease which affects
the leaves, making them look yellow and dead, will
be controlled partly by this same spray. These
are the two diseases that trouble beans. The insect enemies, the flea-beetle and lice, may be controlled by tobacco dust or by spraying.

It will not be long until it will be time to gather
some beans for dinner. After all our care in growing them, we must not fail to pick them when exactly right. We shall need to plan the dinner
usually to suit the garden. Snap beans are ready
just before the beans begin to bulge in the pod. If
left longer, the pods will be tough and stringy,
because, as the bean itself grows, it feeds on the
tenderest part of the cellular tissue. So, the bigger the seed, the tougher the snap beans become.
Gather the beans—all of them—when they are
just right. Whatever you do not need may go to
the neighbors or be put into jars for winter. Picking the beans clean keeps the plants blossoming
and so extends the time of fruitage. Salad beans
should be gathered while very tender. Kidney
beans are ready when the bean is fully formed,
before the shell begins to shrivel. At that stage
of development, the bean has made full use of all
the food supply in the pod. Limas lose their flavor
if they are left as long as the kidneys. Pick the

limas as soon as the beans are barely plump, while the pods are still green. Harvesting at the right time makes a great difference in the flavor of beans.

XIII

BEETS AND CHARD

THE beet is the only vegetable usually grown both for root and foliage. As certain varieties have been developed for table use, the roots have become rounder, growing nearer the surface and so more rapidly; and, at the same time naturally, the tops have grown bigger and tenderer. The long-rooted more slowly growing kinds are being used less and less for the table. One variety, Swiss chard, has been so developed that, like celery, it produces mainly leaves. All kinds are hardy and easy to grow, and all are good for food. The roots are full of starch and the leaves provide the green coarse food so necessary to health. The hardiness of beets makes it possible to grow them early, and the first "thinnings" are ready to help satisfy the spring hunger for green things, long before the main garden is ready.

Beet "seeds," as we consider them, are tiny fruits with hard rough husks, containing, each of them, two or more seeds. Their outer covering is so hard that they are planted shells and all. The seeds are so completely protected by the hard husks that they may be safely kept for five years

or more,—even after that time germinating well.
It is of no advantage to produce beet seed. The
seed comes so true and there are so many good
varieties suited to almost any and every soil and
climate, that one could venture to buy beet seed
at the corner grocery. Certainly it can be secured safely of a reliable seedsman. The round-
rooted kinds, the "turnip varieties," should be
chosen. We will sow, say, the Eclipse for early
beets and the Crimson Globe for later; and, of
course, we must have some Swiss chard.

Beets grow best in sandy loam. However, any
good garden soil will do. Prepare a generous strip
for all the roots on the border of the garden near
the perennials. We decided to keep that strip for
roots as much as possible, allowing, of course, for
occasional rotation to husband the soil food and
to prevent disease. That arrangement is an advantage in order to leave in the ground certain
long-season roots—like salsify and parsnips—
after the main garden has been made ready for
winter. Also, related plants requiring about the
same care may be more conveniently grown together. If the garden has been thoroughly prepared for general planting, it is practically ready
for the beets. Just before sowing, give the entire
strip a careful deep cultivation to make the soil
loose and fine and to get rid of the stones. Disposing of the stones is more important with the
root-crops than with any other, because stones in

IV.—Sweet Corn—Golden Bantam.

the way cause misshapen, rough, branched gnarly roots.

Put in the beets early. If there is room, a few may be grown in the hotbed for the first greens and for a mess or two of little butter-beets. They may be sown in the garden as soon as the ground can be worked. We need not wait for it to become warm and dry, for beets like it cool and wet. The middle of April is not too soon, or even the first, when the spring is early. Cold days do not kill the young plants. Even a spring snow will not destroy them. Yet cold weather retards growth, toughens the vegetable. So the middle of April is early enough, usually. Because of the hard husk, beets are slow to germinate, at best. Dampness in the soil will scarcely affect them. For that reason, soak the "fruits" in warm water. That will aid in softening the tough outside shell. Plant in rows, 12 to 18 inches apart, when cultivation is done by hand; 3 feet between double rows, for horse cultivation. Place the fruits about 1 inch apart, and cover to a depth of about 1 inch. Firm the soil well, that the seed may reach the moisture so much needed. During the spring and very early summer, sow every fortnight. While, as a rule, we will keep the roots together, "companion cropping" may be practiced with beets, growing them between some main-season plant like cabbage. In that way, by repeated sowings, a supply of fresh greens and tender young beets will be ready for use all the time. As the hot weather approaches, discontinue the seeding until fall, because beets need cool moist weather for perfect growth. The winter supply of roots to be stored may be obtained from late summer and early fall sowing. If germination is hastened by soaking the fruits, soon the little clumps of seedlings will be appearing along the rows. In a short time, these clumps will be crowded enough to need thinning; and then the freshest beet greens will be ready. In six weeks, the little butter-beets will be on hand. Two months, usually, will develop the roots at their best.

As soon as the little clumps of beets appear, we will begin to feed them a sprinkle of nitrogen along the row. Feed the plants and cultivate at the same time. The weeds will thus never get a chance, unless now and then one appears in the row among the beets. Such stray weeds must be pulled. Cultivation must be close to the root, tilling deeper as the root grows. The plants depend on the stirring of the soil to secure fresh food and air and to provide much of the moisture so necessary to beets. So keep at it, doing the gardener's part; and watch the beets grow. Do not allow the ground to dry out. Dry-farming is hard on beets. If the weather is dry, the beets, always so thirsty, may need a thorough soaking. The cool water from the hose cannot injure beets, if turned on in the morning. Soak the roots clear down through to the damp lower soil; and, as soon as the surface begins to dry, follow it up with a shallow cultivation to make it last. As soon as the clumps get big enough for greens, begin to thin them. After a time, the roots will start crowding. Then pull enough to give 3 or 4 inches room. More space will make them grow bigger; but they will be coarse in texture and will lose in quality of flavor. Use the thinnings, the smallest plants, roots and all, for greens, "pot-herbs." Make a salad of the tiny beets or use them for butter-beets. If the salad is to be tasty and the greens delicious, there must be continuously rapid growth. Slow growth will mean tough and stringy roots and tasteless greens. Flavor lies in closely packed, quickly filled cells. Feed generously and keep up the cultivation.

When the beets come to maturity, or even with the first thinnings of greens, we will be glad for all the care invested. No greens taste better at that time of the spring than beet greens. They are ready before we stop cutting the asparagus and when the dandelions are getting tough and bitter. Cooked with the tiny beets, when they are fresh and crisp, served with a slice of fried pork or a bit of bacon, they are delicious. As the beets grow a little bigger, like butternuts, they are just right for butter-beets and also for salad. No summer pickle is quite so appetizing as these tiny beets in a sweet pickle. Using the thinnings in these various ways, variety and attractiveness are added to the diet.

All through the year even, the rich red of the beets may garnish the table; their succulent flavor and health-giving mineral salts and the energy stored away in the sweetness of the root may keep the doctor away. Remember to put in plenty of beets; do not forget the late summer sowings and so provide for enough to put into storage. The surplus greens and roots from the early spring crop will furnish plenty to can. The roots may all be stored. However, it is a great convenience to the busy housewife to have a jar ready to heat up, at a minute's notice. It is a big saving in time to prepare a quantity of tender roots, fresh from the garden. They may be gotten ready for canning out-doors in the summer time, with plenty of water from the hose or the well; and it will be much pleasanter work than preparing a little mess of hard partly withered roots each time they are needed. The canning need take no more fuel; and the resulting product is very much better. Both greens and roots are tenderer, when stored in glass jars; they are fresher in flavor and richer in color; and they are all ready to use. In packing the greens after blanching, tuck in around the sides of the glass jar some of the tiny red roots. They can be used to garnish the greens. Cook the beets in the open kettle just long enough to slip off the skins. Use the red blanching water —rich in food elements—to cover the beets and, in that way, keep them from drying out and becoming tough.

One caution may be needed concerning all canned greens. They should be used the first winter. Left over, they soften and may lose color and flavor. The blanching water makes a most healthful basis for a cream soup. If there is too much, more than needed at canning time to fill the jars, boil it down or can the surplus in separate jars. Not a bit should be wasted. To use it for soup, press the left-over greens through a sieve, add the beets finely chopped or ground; season and thicken a little and supper is almost ready. All in all, the very best way to store beets and nearly all vegetables is in glass jars. Only so is the flavor kept really fresh and the texture tender. Lacking jars, they may be dried, both greens and roots. The roots may be buried in a furrow, with the tops down and the soil packed well above them. In mild seasons the beets might weather the cold, left where they grew; but mild seasons are too uncertain to be at all dependable. Next to canning, the best way to store roots is in a cool, moist, dirt-bottomed cellar, laying the roots on the ground. Barrels or boxes of sand will store quite a family supply of beets; and they will keep fairly firm and crisp, if the sand is moist.

Swiss chard.—A special word may be said concerning Swiss chard or the chard or leaf-beet. Its growth differs so much from the ordinary table beet that it is classed among the "pot-herb crops." It has been so carefully bred for salad foliage and for greens that now, like celery or spinach, it is almost entirely foliage. The big, broad, light green, thick succulent leaves are supported by tough branched roots, just large enough to balance the heavy top and provide the necessary sustenance. Its luxuriant growth, unhindered by the heat, continues throughout the entire summer and for this reason furnishes a most excellent supplement to spinach, for the latter cannot endure midsummer heat.

The Swiss chard is ready for use when the early spinach and the beet thinnings are gone; and, when cared for, will keep on furnishing the tenderest greens all summer long. Sow the Swiss chard seeds about 4 inches apart, thinning as the plants grow, until they stand no less than 16 inches apart. This will allow plenty of room for the biggest growth. Only one sowing need be made, for, as we know, Swiss chard is an all-season vegetable. Feed at least twice as much nitrogen as would be given to the other varieties. Treat Swiss chard as a foliage plant, apply nitrogen freely, give it plenty of water and keep stirring the soil. Such care will insure big crisp leaves. As soon as the leaves are large enough to use, begin to pick the outer ones for greens. Keep on cutting the outside leaves as they grow, and the big plants will keep on growing, all the season through. In time the leaves will be so large that the thickened leaf-stem may be used in salad like celery, or cooked like asparagus. Then the outer leaf-blades are stripped from the midrib and used as greens. Try blanching some of the plants by tying close together the big leaf clusters. After a short time, you will find the hearts white and crisp and delicate of flavor, ready to be used fresh with other vegetables as a cool tempting salad.

The more Swiss chard is fed and tended, the bigger and crisper will the plants become. They will keep on growing until long after frost. I have found fresh green leaves even until Christmas. The light snow had heaped over the row; and there had been no wind to blow the plants bare. So until the "January thaw," for just the bother of pushing away the drift, there was plenty of fresh crisp greens at the heart of the plants. Some care will be needed to protect the growing beets, all of the varieties, from enemies and disease. Tobacco dust will keep away the fleas and the leaf-miner, the worst enemies of the beet.

XIV

BRUSSELS SPROUTS

GROWING brussels sprouts is much like raising miniature cabbages. The sprouts appear as axillary buds at the juncture of each leaf with the strong straight stem. As the plant grows, these sprouts keep appearing all along the stem, until, at the top, a bunch of loose leaves spreads out like a canopy over the stalk of tiny cabbages. A good sprout measures from 1 to 2 inches across and is solid and hard and of a rather light green color. Some varieties grow from 2 to 3 feet high. Other dwarf kinds measure only about 18 inches, with sprouts of corresponding size. While they seem to thrive best in a seashore climate, like Long Island, they also will grow well in inland gardens and are suited to a short-season climate. Wherever they are grown for home use, they are much prized for their attractive appearance and juicy tenderness and fine flavor, being considered the most delicate of all the members of the cabbage family.

With brussels sprouts everything depends on the strain of seed. The plants tend to run down, to revert to the old type of growth. Therefore, the greatest care is needed in the production and selection of seed. While we can easily test for germination, the real trial of this vegetable does not come until maturity; the proof of brussels sprouts is surely in the eating. As a rule, there is no advantage to the home gardener in attempting to produce seed from biennial vegetables, even when the climate makes it possible. A package of Dalkeith brussels sprouts or other carefully selected strain will afford the best possible start.

This vegetable is especially prized in late fall and early winter. For that reason, seeds are sown rather late, in order that they may not mature too early. The best most succulent growth is made in the moist cool late summer. Brussels sprouts is essentially a fall crop. Sow in the hotbed, or in a finely prepared somewhat shaded seed-bed, in June in a climate about like central New York or any of the middle states. The seeds should be scattered less than ½ inch apart, in a furrow ½ inch deep. The germination test is an aid in determining how much to vary the direction given for distance in sowing any seed. The poorer the percentage of germination, the closer the seeds should be placed.

A word of direction concerning the method of sowing might help the inexperienced gardener. Empty the packet of seeds into a shallow saucer. Take a pinch between the thumb and first finger and, as the hand is moved over the tiny furrow, work the seed off by rubbing the end of the thumb lightly over the finger. If, at first, the seed gets scattered too thickly, take a pinch, here and there, dirt and all, and scatter it farther along in the furrow. Better sow too thickly than too far apart. The value of even expensive seed is of little account when the final success of the crop is concerned. As soon as the seeds start, it is easy to pinch out the extra ones, if the seedlings are crowded.

With the proper care, continual stirring of the soil and plenty of moisture, a month or six weeks will find the little sprouts ready to transplant. By that time, the second set of real leaves will have appeared and the cotyledons withered, yellowed, nearly disappeared. Be careful not to get the cabbage seedlings instead, for these young related plants are very much alike. Choose a cloudy moist day for transplanting. A deep, rich, even loam is best; but any soil suitable for general gardening will grow fine brussels sprouts. Have the soil in the strip freshly cultivated and ready when the plants are removed from the seed-bed. Lift only a few at a time and keep the lump of soil around the seedlings moist.

The subsequent care of brussels sprouts is simple. The plants may need shading, the first few days, during the hottest part of the day. Push a stick into the soil at a little distance from each plant and over the stick and the plant pin a newspaper. It may be easier to lay the papers over the measuring line tied well above the tops of the plants. After a time, if the weather is dry, they will need watering; and, for seedlings newly set, always use water that is warm enough so that the tender plants will not be chilled and thus growth checked. Continual stirring of the soil must be kept up. Feed the little cabbages a bit of nitrate every ten days and, as this stimulant is distributed, cultivate. As the heads begin to crowd, some of the leaves should be broken to give more room. Always leave the sheltering canopy untouched, because, unless shaded, the delicate flavor may be injured and the buds acquire their original strong cabbage flavor.

We may expect the harvest in four months or a little over. When sown in June, we may look for mature sprouts all through October and November. The biggest buds are gathered as needed, leaving the plants to go on developing the sprouts. Be sure to gather in the early morning, if you want to keep them fresh and full of flavor.

The plants are left out all winter in mild climates. Where the winter weather is freezing, they are dug late in the fall and stored. They may be kept fresh for winter use in such localities by digging up the mature plants and placing them root down close together in a pit below the frost line or in a coldframe or a cool cellar. If soil is scattered about the roots, enough moisture and sustenance may be secured to keep the sprouts fairly crisp. As the weather grows colder, added protection against freezing is needed. It may be of interest to note that we usually store all foliage plants "right side up" for the very same reason that we store root-crops "up-side-down." With beets and other roots stored for winter use, the procedure is to keep the tops from growing, while with all foliage plants the opposite result is desired. Growth of the tops is at the expense of firmness and crispness and flavor of the roots, because as the roots furnish moisture and sustenance to the foliage, they shrink and shrivel and consequently lose flavor. With foliage plants, the hard gnarly roots are merely a means of growth. So our brussels sprouts are to be placed as they grew naturally, depending on the roots, as they take a little hold on the soil, to secure moisture and food enough to keep the baby cabbages fairly crisp and fresh.

Like all vegetables, the sprouts may be canned. If they are stored in this way, one or two suggestions may be of value. Plunge the blanching basketful of fresh sprouts into boiling water for a minute and then for another minute into cold water to preserve the fresh color. When they are packed, use fresh water to fill the glass jars. When the jars are opened, the water may be kept for soup if the flavor is still fresh. With all of the cabbage varieties, although the water in which they are cooked is rich in mineral salts and so may frugally be used as a basis for soup, still it often loses flavor when canned, after the jars have stood for some time. Whatever is done with the blanching water, the sprouts, whether fresh or canned, are sure to taste good. Cook until tender and drain. Then toss them about in some melted butter, salt and pepper a bit, or put them in a pickle.

Brussels sprouts are easy to grow. They need no special place in the garden plan. They may be tucked in as a companion crop with lettuce or pole-beans or among the big summer squashes. The squashes and the beans would shade them; and, if plenty of food were furnished, they would do well there. They will grow well almost anywhere as a second crop. They might follow the first crop of beets. Since they are foliage plants, we may expect them to grow best, however, after the legumes. They are far more attractive and delicate than cabbage; hardier, they are ready for use when all other green vegetables are gone.

XV

CABBAGE

GREAT care is needed in the selection of cabbage seed. Germination of all round seeds depends less on their being "fresh" than on the year in which they were grown. So, in buying these seeds, we especially need reliability in our seedsman. For early cabbage, no variety is better than the Early Jersey Wakefield. For a late cabbage, we might choose the Autumn King. It is unusually large and hard and sweet. If you wish to try a Savoy cabbage, grow it with the late varieties, choosing the Drumhead Savoy. Its crumpled leaves are very tender and delicious after the frost has touched them. Red Dutch seed will grow excellent hard-headed red cabbage.

For an extra prime crop, early seeding is especially imperative. This and the proper care of the young plants are the main factors, if the soil is suitable. The seed should be sown at least ten weeks before planting in the garden. Young cabbage plants are not injured by the frost or even by heavy freezing when grown properly. To have sturdy plants for April, we might well put in the seeds as early as the first of February. They may be sown in the hotbed or in pans or boxes in the kitchen window. That is a more convenient place to tend them, in February weather. In about a month, early in March, our young cabbages will be ready for their first transplanting. By that time, they will no longer need the tender hotbed care, if they have not been forced or hurried in their growth. They should then be straight and strong and stocky. Remove them from the kitchen window-boxes to a coldframe that may be merely a glass-covered frame set over a warm spot in the garden. Pinch the leaf ends a little, each time they are moved, in order to turn the plant vigor towards root growth at first. Harden the young plants gradually by removing the sash of glass farther and longer each day. If they are short and stocky in stem and the leaves have a reddish blue tinge, the plants are surely ready for the open garden.

Cabbage may be adapted to almost any garden soil. A sandy loam hastens maturity; a rather heavy sandy loam, well-drained and yet heavy enough to hold its full of moisture, deep and cool and thoroughly and evenly prepared, is an ideal cabbage soil. Now for the setting. Place them from 18 inches to 2 feet from each other in rows 2 to 3 feet apart. Provided it is thoroughly watered, almost no plant transplants so well as cabbage. Taking the plant in the left hand, make the opening beneath the measuring line with the right hand, and put in a little tobacco dust, and a bit of bone-meal. As the plant is placed in position, pinch the leaf ends a bit, press back the earth around the roots and then, with both hands, firm the soil well. Then water, using enough to soak the soil thoroughly. A quart is not too much unless the ground is very moist. In a few days, they will probably need more water. Shading the plants at first during the middle of the day will keep them from wilting by preventing evaporation from the leaves. If all the young plants are not ready for the open garden at the same time, it may be an advantage. Transplanting a few at a time will lengthen the harvest. With such care in the early growth of the seedlings and in transplanting, we should have plants hardy enough to resist unhurt even freezing weather and vigorous enough to produce big, hard, tender heads of sweet cabbage.

The subsequent care means tillage and food and water. Continuous growth from seedling to harvest is most essential. Interrupted stunted growth means poor heads. Few plants are stronger or grow more rapidly than cabbage when cared for. Few are more sensitive to neglect. If growth is checked when the plants begin to head and then started into fresh growth by renewed care, there is danger of cracked heads. Loosening the roots slightly with a spading fork is said to check cracking. Steady persistent cultivation, however, is an almost sure prevention of this difficulty. Frequent surface tillage is a certain protection against drought and furnishes a steady supply of moisture. Cultivation means everything. Keep at it as long as there is room between the plants. Cabbages are great feeders; they have voracious appetites, and must have an extra supply of nitrogenous food. That will be distributed regularly as cultivation goes on. The bone-meal beneath the roots will supply the additional phosphorus needed to make hard heads. An abundance of quickly available food supply is essential to the harvest. If the weather is very dry, it may be necessary to water the cabbages; but an even supply of the moisture furnished by steady cultivation is much better than a thorough soaking followed by a bone-dry spell. However, water the cabbages when necessary; do it in thorough fashion; and follow it with shallow tillage to form the surface moisture-conserving mulch. Uninterrupted growth from hot-bed to harvest is the one prime requisite in growing cabbage.

Protection from disease and garden enemies will be especially necessary. Club-root, root-maggot and black-rot are the principal pests of the cabbage. Careful rotation must be practiced and cabbage should not be planted for several years on infested land. The cabbage worm may be controlled by an arsenate of lead bordeaux spray, until the plants begin to head.

The time of harvesting garden cabbages depends on when the head is firm and hard and big enough. A hard cabbage is solid and firm throughout; the outside leaves have done their work of blanching the heart and so making it tender and sweet and crisp. Cut the head early in the morning and keep it where it is cool. This is absolutely essential if it is to be used fresh as a salad. Nothing is so tasteless, so disappointing as a wilted salad. Preparing it early helps to keep any salad fresh and crisp. Put the shredded cabbage in a cheese-cloth bag in the ice-chest, on the ice itself if we are sure the ice is clean and pure enough for food. Keep it cool somewhere; and whatever the dressing, the salad will be good. Whether used in salads or cooked, any vegetable must be gathered while fresh and kept fresh until it is put over to cook. Wilted vegetables lose much in crispness and flavor. Some of the early morning freshness may be restored by putting them into cold water for a while before cooking. Plunging into the cold water stiffens the cellular tissue, plumps the partly dried starch cells of the roots, and freshens the leaves. It restores crispness and partially brings back the flavor. No one needs telling how corned-beef and cabbage are prepared. That is a dish as well-known, almost as widely used, I presume, as the cabbage is widely grown. For that dish, the corned-beef must be first class. Then, if the cabbage is cooked right, there will be nothing left over when dinner is done. Keep the cabbage steaming until it is tender. Over-cooked cabbage grows dark and loses its succulent flavor. Serve it, well-salted and hot, while it is still creamy white and tender and sweet. If cabbage is boiled, the water, so full of health-giving mineral salts, may be used for a cream soup.

Cabbage may easily be kept over the winter, so that we may have this succulent vegetable nearly the year round. There is one advantage in canning the cabbage in the fall for winter use. It does away with the unpleasant cooking odor, especially objectionable when cabbage is cooked in winter. Canned cabbage, however, is not quite so good; the flavor may become stale. The best way to keep cabbages for winter is to store them in pits. Make a trench at least 1 foot deep and 4 feet wide. Make certain that no water has collected in the heads. Pack the cabbages, heads down, leaving all the soil possible on the roots and removing no leaves. The heavy outside leaves wrapped closely together about the head will in themselves preserve the freshness of the heart of the cabbage. Cover with a little straw and, over the straw covering, place a scattering of earth. As the weather grows colder, add more earth, until after hard freezing weather has come, there will be a foot of earth over the cabbage-pit. The pit may be opened at one end, whenever the cabbage is needed. Whether fresh or stored, this homely everyday vegetable so common and yet, in its varied forms so unusual, is seen on everybody's table and eaten with equal relish by "the high and the lowly."

XVI

CARROTS

FOR many years the carrot has been used to feed the stock; but only recently have we come to appreciate its value as a nutritious and appetizing food. When grown in the fields to feed the cattle, large long-rooted varieties are chosen: and an entire season is allowed for complete growth. To secure large yields of fully developed big roots, tenderness and flavor have to be sacrificed. For table use, we select small-sized varieties, those that come quickly to maturity. By that means, with the proper care, the tender crispness and the delicate flavor are preserved. The small carrot that develops quickly is less liable to the hard tough core always found in the big stock-feed vegetable. These small carrots do not usually crack; the uniform texture from center to outside prevents cracking and keeps the surface smooth. The Half Long Danvers is considered an excellent variety. The Coreless is shorter and somewhat smaller than the Danvers, very uniform in shape and size, with a smooth clean skin, and a rich orange color. It actually has no core, when grown properly; it is crisp clear through and meltingly tender and delicate in flavor. The Coreless carrot is also a spring-time product; the best table carrots are always grown in the cool spring.

Carrots grow best in well-drained sandy loam. Heavy, lumpy, stony soil, however rich, will produce rough misshapen roots. The soil must be made clean and even in texture by deep fine preparation to break up the clods and get rid of the stones and lighten the texture. No tool is so deft as the potato hook. Give the soil a dressing of wood-ashes and work it in as the ground is made ready. The nitrate stimulant may be used on the surface along the rows, just after growth starts; but the potash (in the wood-ashes) is not so quickly available and needs, also, to be deeper in the soil. Therefore, work in the ashes as the soil is prepared for sowing.

The time for sowing carrots is as early as the ground can be made ready, clean and mellow and fine. Then lay out the rows, from 1 to 2 feet apart; 1 foot will do, if space is limited. Because of low vitality, the seed must be sown more thickly. Sometimes, only about one-fifth of those sown will start. It is well to sow at least four seeds to the inch. Because of their slow germination, the surface is likely to break and crack before the delicate seedlings appear. Sometimes because of their lack of vigor, they are unable to break through the crust. Together with the carrot seed sow some sort of strong quickly germinating seed, like radish. Scatter the two sorts together and cover only about ½ inch. The vigorous radish seeds will start more quickly and so the surface will be kept soft and open, providing a fair start for the weaker carrot seedlings.

Once started, there is no difficulty in growing perfect carrots. 'Cultivation may begin before the seedlings appear, even before germination. As soon as the radishes begin to show enough to mark the row, tillage may begin; the weeds in the seed row may be nipped. Scatter a little nitrate far enough away so that there may be no danger of burning the young growth just germinating. Keep the soil between the rows stirred to conserve the food and to prevent a crust forming. The carrot seedlings are shallow-rooted and delicate at first. Care will be especially needed just as they are starting. As the surface is stirred, work the soil a little towards the seedlings to help anchor the frail roots. When only an inch high, growth will be hastened and made more vigorous by thinning the tiny plants to ¾ inch apart, the width of your thumb. Go down the row, measuring the space between by your thumb, as you pull out the tiny crowding plants. At the same time, with the same live tools, press the soil closely about those that are left to grow. After this, growth should be constant and rapid. Keep the soil stirred. When the growing carrots are as large as your thumb, thin them again, this time leaving them

2 or 3 inches apart. Too much room makes them
bigger and coarser, not so delicate and tender as
the slender deeper growing roots. Now all that
remains is tillage. As the roots grow, cultivate
deeper and, at the same time, work the soil over
the row to keep the bulging crowns from becoming
sun-burned and, therefore, dark and bitter. If
they are left bare, they are liable also to crack.
Keep the crowns covered and make room for the
roots to grow.

There are no enemies worth considering. A
white mildewy fungus causes soft-rot, sometimes,
when the roots are stored. The riddance of this
fungus is best effected by carefully destroying all
roots having the least sign of the rot, in order to
prevent the fungus from becoming lodged in the
soil. When left in the ground after maturity, a
little yellow wireworm tunnels its way into the
surface and spoils the smooth appearance of the
roots. Continual cultivation to secure early maturity prevents any injury from this borer; that
is, if the crop is then harvested. With such attention, we may be assured of plenty of smooth
tender roots, glowing in color and delicious in
flavor.

The carrot harvest is a movable feast. It may
begin as soon as the roots are large enough and
the color is rich enough for a salad. Start with
the thumb-sized roots pulled to provide more room.
They will make a delicious salad. Carrots fed to

the horse give him a glossy skin and make him step high, they say. While the carrots are small and crisp, we will have raw carrot salad. Lay a bunch of the slender rich salmon-colored roots on the white cool heart of a lettuce head. Garnish with the feathery tops. Salt them a bit and eat them like radishes, every day. As they grow bigger, their delicate flavor will change somewhat and the texture will become a little less crisp. Then cook them till tender and brown them in butter, garnishing with their own tops or with parsley. Plan to serve them, in this way, when company comes. Have a plain lettuce salad, too, and spread a fresh white cloth. Nothing else will matter much, unless we need a bunch of variegated nasturtiums with their leaves in the center. Whatever else we may have will surely taste good, for the unconscious harmony of color itself is refreshing and heartening and serves as a real appetizer.

There's another and most practical use of this favorite root that we like to recall—the old days when the golden yellow carrot juice made the white winter butter just like the fresh new butter of June. However we may use this most useful root, be sure to allow none to waste. Every one will be delicious, cooked until tender and then browned in butter or some bacon fat. Be sure to turn off the water in which they were cooked and save it for soup; it is full of the mineral salts that help so much to bring fresh color and new zest.

Chopped carrots make a very good cream soup with chopped onions. Cook each vegetable until tender and finish them together with a thin cream sauce and some minced parsley stirred in and some grated cheese sprinkled over the top. No vegetable is so satisfactory canned; none keeps its fresh flavor and firm texture so well or so long. In canning, treat them like beets, except for the difference in the skin. The thin skin may be allowed to remain unless the carrots are fully matured. After blanching, it may improve the appearance to rub off the skin before packing. Then sterilize and put away for the time of need. Planning to can them makes it possible to grow the entire crop in the spring, the season when we are sure of the tenderest, best flavored, cleanest roots. If canning the surplus is inadvisable, then the winter supply should be matured late in the fall and stored in a dry cool cellar, in sand.

XVII

CAULIFLOWER

AT first thought, one might suppose that the culture of cauliflower would be much like that of brussels sprouts; but there are real differences that must be considered, if we would succeed in growing perfect heads. Instead of a lot of tiny cabbages for each stalk, we have, as the result of our labors, one head on a stalk. The harvest then depends on the size and quality of these heads. They are less strong of flavor than cabbage and far more delicate and attractive. The cauliflowers of New York state are mostly furnished by Long Island. The moist air with the cool nights of Long Island and the same climatic conditions in the Great Lakes region and about Puget Sound are especially favorable to the best growth of this vegetable so dependent on climate for perfection of growth. It is difficult to grow perfect cauliflower; a moist river valley is preferable to a hillside and the humid climate of the coast to an inland garden. However, with intelligent persistent care, good cauliflowers may be grown in any home garden.

It is vitally important at the outset to secure

the best seed. No other vegetable seems to run down so quickly from poor seed. Too much emphasis, therefore, cannot be placed on buying the very best. That means, again, reliance on our seedsman, for it certainly does not pay to try to produce our own cauliflower seeds, unless as a bit of an adventure to see what happens. The best seed has for many years been obtained from Denmark, although much excellent seed is being produced now by Puget Sound growers. Dwarf Erfurt and Snowball may be chosen as the finest for early varieties, Snowball being somewhat earlier. Broccoli is merely a hardy late-maturing sort of cauliflower. For a late variety, Sea Foam is suggested. The plants may be grown in the latter part of the season; but it is best to start them as early as possible in the spring, while the weather is cool and moist and the sunshine not yet hot.

Good heads may be grown in a great variety of gardens. Let us try our first cauliflower as an early crop, getting them in as far as possible ahead of the dry weather. Grown as a first crop, they have full use of the early supply of moisture so thoroughly distributed in the soil; they have the abundant food supply made ready during the fallow winter months; and, during these early spring weeks, the soil is cool. The atmosphere is more humid then. Therefore, as amateurs in growing this uncertain crop, our best chances for success

V.—WATERMELONS.—"They are handsome fruits to grow."

come in the spring. Sow in the hotbed as early
as the first of April, perhaps a little later, depending on the season. Scatter the seeds less than
½ inch apart, following the detailed directions
given for brussels sprouts, in both sowing and
transplanting. With April seeding, the young
plants should be ready for setting out by the middle of May. Special care as to moisture and even-
ness of temperature is needed for cauliflower
seedlings more than for any other vegetable, while
in the hotbed. Resetting the young plants once
before transplanting into the open garden is said
to make them stronger. In my experience, thus
far, there has been no difficulty in starting sturdy
young plants. Keep the hotbed in an even spring
temperature and provide a steady supply of air
and moisture; try to have the hotbed like a little
garden. The plants should then make a normal,
rapid, sturdy growth and be ready for the out-
doors early in May. Take special care to choose a
cool, moist, cloudy day for transplanting; and put
them out exactly as brussels sprouts. Plants may
be secured of a neighboring nurseryman to supplement our own supply.

If, to lengthen the cauliflower season, we decide
to grow late varieties, in addition to the early
kinds, plan to start them as late as possible, allowing time for maturity before danger of real
frost. Cauliflower does not withstand frost like
brussels sprouts and cabbage. Find out from the

weather forecasts when a real frost may be expected; allow about six weeks for seed-bed growth and another six weeks until maturity, and put in the seeds accordingly. For late cauliflower, the seed may be sown in a shady place in the garden in finely prepared soil. Provide plenty of moisture; and, if necessary, extra shade may be furnished by means of a loosely woven cheese-cloth cover stretched tightly well above the final height of the seedlings (say, 8 or 9 inches) and fastened securely to corner and middle stakes. By that means, the tender young plants may be shaded during the hottest part of the day, the cover being removed when the air becomes cool and moist.

Sturdy young plants must be kept sturdy if, for each plant, we are to harvest a perfect head of cauliflower. Rapid, steady, uniform growth is necessary. The plants *must* have plenty of water if they are to be kept in a condition of thrift. There is no need to emphasize the necessity of continual surface tillage. The season itself will have much to do with the result. A cool damp summer is an advantage. Wet weather, with little sunshine, at the time of heading will be a great aid. If the weather is hot and dry at that critical time or if growth has been retarded, we shall have, instead of smooth compact heads, "buttons," irregular growths, a kind of broken-up head. Poor seed will also produce buttons, showing that the plants are turning back, reverting to the uncultivated type of growth. These buttons are tough and bitter and green, useless as food. Care is especially needed to prevent this difficulty. As soon as the heads are 1½ inches in diameter, begin to protect them from the heat and sunshine. The heat causes the buttons and the bright sunshine turns the growing heads green. To cool and shade the forming buds, a few of the top leaves are partially broken and bent over the plant. They may then be pinned together with tooth-picks to keep them in place. Sometimes, instead of breaking the leaves, tie them together over the plant. Either plan will do so long as the young buds are kept shaded well while developing. Even though compact heads should form, uncovered, the heat and sunshine are sure to render them coarse and tough and dark colored and bitter. Sun-burn spoils the heads. Covering them is like blanching; it produces a creamy white color and a delicate flavor. Be sure to provide plenty of water and keep the soil stirred.

Little attention need be given to protection against disease and live enemies. Tobacco takes care of cutworms; a good hosing will drive off the lice and the worms and cool the plants. Little care will be needed in that direction.

To succeed with cauliflower, the gardener needs simply to have first-class seed; uniform growth to produce sturdy plants; careful patient attention to keep the plants cool and moist and shaded

and constantly growing. Unless a steady dry hot
season is against his efforts, he may be fairly sure
of a satisfactory harvest. This means an almost
snowy white, compact, hard, smooth, delicately
flavored head for each plant. If sown in April,
some of the cauliflowers will mature by the first
of July. Of course, the time varies with the season. From July on for some time cauliflower may
provide variety and attractiveness for the home
table. The proper time to pick these flower-buds
is just before the bud begins to open. They may
be eaten boiled and served with a cream sauce.
They are an essential in "mustard pickle." They
are very good pickled alone. The surplus may be
canned but the blanching and packing must be
done very quickly, else they will grow dark. Some
of the late crop may be stored, although the result
is loss of flavor and freshness of color, at best.
Storing cauliflower is not very satisfactory. Let
the neighbors use the surplus during the season
and, in that way, add to the pleasure of growing
them.

XVIII

CELERY

CELERY may be grown by anybody, almost anywhere. Ideal climatic conditions, however, require bright sunshine, pure air, cool nights, even rainfall. Rich, mellow, well-drained sandy loam is ideal soil for garden celery. The largest part of the market crop is produced on the heavy fertile soil of river-bottoms or in the muck-bed areas of lake regions. Such moist peat-bog lands produce the biggest most succulent growth. The celery thus grown does not have quite so fine a flavor, however, and does not keep so well as that grown on looser, more sandy, upland soil. For the home supply, excellent celery may be grown in any fruitful, well-drained, well-cared-for soil, even clay. Add to the clay, the fall before, plenty of humus and well-rotted manure; keep the surface continually stirred during growth, to prevent packing; watch out after a hard heavy rain to see that this pasty soil, when washed into the hearts of the young plants, does not smother new growth; and with proper care, even clay will grow excellent celery. Red pasty clay may be made over into almost ideal soil; but loose, well-drained sandy loam is to be preferred.

For the best results, any soil must have careful preparation. The fall and spring care of our garden has already made the soil nearly suited for successful celery growing. In its fall preparation, plenty of humus was provided and also a generous supply of well-rotted manure. Both were incorporated in the soil when it was plowed. The spring preparation furnished a thorough dressing of the highest grade commercial fertilizer, 4-8-10 being used. It will be an advantage for celery to follow some soil-enriching crop like early peas. When the peas have been harvested and the celery strip is fitted, about a week before the plants are ready to be set, additional food may well be supplied. Celery profits by potash and nitrogen. A 6-5-10 mixture, therefore, would be correct. Experiments have shown that wood-ashes are the best potash provider for celery. With that, sodium nitrate works well. We might use, instead of the 6-5-10, a dressing of unleached ashes and some nitrate along the celery strip. Whichever is chosen, work the fertilizer into the row, in a strip about 18 inches wide. Salt was put on in the fall. More may be scattered on the ground when it is freshly cultivated just before planting time. Some of the salt is said to be taken up by the growing celery and the flavor thereby improved.

We must buy the best and the freshest celery seed. We may decide, instead, to start with plants. In that case, arrange with your market-gardener, and have the celery strip ready when the plants are to be delivered. Such a plan is an easier shorter cut to the celery harvest and, for the first year of gardening, it may be best. If we start with seed, we must have the freshest from selected stock, true to name. Choose the seedsman that has had the most experience in the culture of celery seed, a business in itself. Be willing to pay the highest price, for price alone is a good guarantee of quality; order early, before the freshest best seed is out of stock.

There is a large number of varieties suited to season and to taste. Suppose we choose Golden Self-blanching for the early crop. It is short and stocky in growth; the stalks are broad and thick and crisp; an unusually large heart, tender and rich in flavor. Perhaps we had rather try White Plume. That variety is more slender in growth; brittle-crisp in texture; and delicious in flavor. It is more attractive as a garnish. For the winter supply, we may select a slower growing kind, Golden Dwarf or Boston Market for dwarf varieties and Giant Pascal for big tall-growing plants. All are excellent varieties and will bring satisfaction.

For the early crop, start the seeds in February or March. The best plan for the first seeding is to use trays, broad, shallow wooden boxes with about 16x24 inches of surface and 3 inches deep, boring several small holes in the bottom for drainage. The soil should be leaf-mold mixed with sandy loam, although any fertile garden soil may be used. Run this mixture through a wire sieve with an ⅛-inch mesh; fill the trays; and level off and press the soil down with a bit of board. The seed should then be sown thick in tiny half-inch furrows 2 inches apart, or scattered evenly on the surface. Sift over them a little of the leaf-mold and sand mixture, not more than ⅛ inch deep, just barely to cover the weak seeds. Place the tray in the window of a moderately warm or cool room. During the two weeks or so before the seedlings start, maintain an even soil-moisture. Too much water will puddle the soil and rot the seed. The dry air of the room or drafts blowing across the surface bake the soil and so hinder germination. To insure constant dampness on the surface, by preventing evaporation, a wet cloth or several thicknesses of soaked newspapers may be spread over the top of the tray. Keeping this cover moist by sprinkling, once a day, will be all that is needed. Take a look beneath, now and then. When the seedlings begin to appear, the question of moisture is even more important, and air and light must be considered as well. The tiny plants must be only slightly damp. Too much water sprinkled over them, at once, after allowing the soil to dry out, will cause the frail stems to rot just where they come through the soil. This danger of damping-off may be avoided easily by an even supply of moisture. Sub-watering has been suggested, merely setting the trays in a trough with an inch of water in the bottom. The soil in the tray absorbs the water through the drainage holes, thus providing plenty of water for the roots and yet leaving the surface soil dry. While the seedlings are young and fragile, water may still be supplied by sprinkling through a loosely woven cloth. This cloth should be removed, between times, because fresh air and light must also be provided, if the tender seedlings are to become sturdy plants. Turn the tray about once a day, before the window, to prevent them from drawing towards the light; and, by this means, keep them growing straight and sturdy.

For the late crop for winter use, the seed may be sown in trays like the early seed-bed or in the hotbed or coldframe, or in the garden itself. The weather will be favorable for out-door seeding by the first of May in an average season in central New York. By the time the seedlings appear, the air will be sufficiently warm. Make the seed-bed in a moist place in the garden. Have the soil finely pulverized and uniform in texture; the surface in perfect tilth. Shallow lines, not over ½ inch deep, are then marked across the bed, far enough apart for cultivating with a narrow hook or hoe.

The seed may be scattered broadcast; but that makes the care of the plants more difficult. Sow thickly along the lines, pat the rows down with the hoe or press a narrow board along them. Soil may be sifted over the surface instead; but this slight firming hurries germination a bit. Some gardeners even run the lawn-roller over the bed.

To maintain a moist surface, the bed may be covered with something rather light and loosely woven. Old burlap bagging works well for that purpose. Watering the bagging itself with the garden sprinkler moistens the surface and maintains an evenly moist condition of the whole bed. Watch closely. As soon as germination begins, the cover should be raised, not removed entirely at first. Instead, raise the bagging above the surface on stakes driven close enough to prevent sagging. That will furnish shade for the young plants when needed and protect the frail growth from hard rain or sudden winds. Gradually, as the tiny plants develop, the burlap cover is removed. Meanwhile, the plants may still be watered through the bagging. Whether started in trays or in the hotbed or the garden, whether for the early crop or for winter use, the same care is needed to prevent damping-off or stem-rot. Provide an unvarying supply of moisture; protect the young plants from sudden changes; keep the soil stirred and the weeds nipped; and in about six weeks the healthly seedlings will be ready to transplant.

Young celery plants are, at best, so frail that they should be transplanted once or twice before they are set permanently. To save time, when large quantities are grown, some gardeners merely thin the plants in the seed-bed, setting them when first transplanted where they are to mature. This plan may be necessary when time and help are more valuable than are the plants; but it is a poor policy in the home garden. The celery seedling has naturally a slender tap-root. The first transplanting breaks this sole root and starts a fresh growth of root fibers. Each handling increases the root growth until, finally, the plant has a large mass of fibrous root to furnish sustenance. When thinning is practiced, the weakest plants are pulled and those intended for production of the celery crop are left in the seed-bed until time for setting. During that time, the tap-root keeps growing long and remains simply a single root. When the plants are finally removed to the permanent row and these single roots are broken, the shock is too great for the delicate plants and many of them die. At best, they recover slowly. The twice handled plants with their stocky root growth make quick recovery on setting and produce by far the best results.

When an inch or two high and large enough to get hold of easily, the celery seedlings are ready for their first handling. The tray-grown early plants may then be moved to the hotbed or to other trays of fresh soil. This time, mix some well-rotted manure with the leaf-mold and sand; and sift the mixture less fine. A convenient device for marking the rows and at the same time making the holes is a straight stick with projecting pegs attached at the correct distances for setting the plants, say 2 inches. This dibber-like contrivance may be used to advantage in setting all very small plants. Be sure the seed-bed is wet clear through. Then, before the plants are lifted, loosen the soil in the trays by slipping a flat trowel or a pan-cake turner down the sides and beneath the soil. Take a handful of seedlings, snip off the tips of the top leaves; nip the tap-roots to an inch in length; slip the tiny plants into the holes with the stem no farther below the surface than when in the seed-bed. Press the soil firmly about the frail plants to hold them erect until new growth has begun.

Practically the same plan is followed in handling the later grown plants in the garden seed-bed. Give the same care to the making of the transplanting bed as to the preparation of the soil when the seeds were sown. Wet the seed-bed well before the tiny plants are removed. As soon as the handling is finished, attention will be needed, at first, to shade the plants. After new growth has begun, the experience gained in the care of the seed-bed plants will be nearly all that is needed.

The same attention must be given to furnish an even supply of moisture, to insure steady healthy growth and so prevent damping-off. The plants must be kept cool. For those in the trays, plenty of fresh air will be needed. For those in the open ground, protection against driving wind and hard rain will be provided by using the burlap bagging. Tillage will now be needed. It must be shallow, for the root tendrils of celery plants like to run close to the surface. Stir the top soil often between the rows to keep out the weeds and to hold the moisture up close to the tiny foragers. Such attention will insure healthy steady growth until our inch-high frail seedlings have become robust and sturdy.

When the celery plants are 4 or 5 inches in height, if they should still be rather frail, a second handling might be an advantage. If, however, they are stocky and dark green in color, they are ready for setting in the permanent row. Provide plenty of room, all that can be spared; and stake the rows from 3 to 5 feet apart. Five feet between the rows will allow us to choose any process of blanching. The celery strip has just been freshly fitted and is all ready. For this last handling, choose a damp showery day, if possible. Between showers is an ideal time. Soak the soil thoroughly in the seedling or handling bed a few hours before lifting the plants. Raise them carefully with the sticky wet earth attached to the roots, and lay them in little piles along the row. If the sun should shine out and the air become dry, keep the plants covered in a shallow basket or a tray. Place the early plants 4 inches apart in the row. The later varieties with bigger growth need more room, 5 to 6 inches or even more. Set them no deeper than they were in the bed. Press the soil firmly about the roots, taking pains that it does not get into the heart. Mulching is considered an especial advantage in growing celery.

After the first handling, if the young celery plants are thrifty, they will feed near the surface; that is, if the water supply is evenly distributed so that the soil is moist to the top. Otherwise, like all roots, they will work deeper as the upper soil dries. The best feeding-ground is near the top, because there the soil is more perfectly aërated and plant-food is becoming most quickly available. Therefore, the best means must be used to induce fibrous roots like celery to feed high. The dust mulch is an advantage, because that hinders evaporation and renders the soil fairly evenly moist. A mulch of some loose material spread over the soil does more; it shades the surface and keeps it cool and, thus preventing evaporation, holds the moisture clear to the top of the ground. For this special mulch, lawn clippings or ground corn-stalks or well-rotted strawy manure are recommended. Have a basketful or a pile near by. As the plants are set, spread the mulch evenly

over a 10-inch strip on each side of the row. Bring
it close to the plants; but do not allow a particle
to get into the delicate heart. After the plants
are all set and the mulch distributed, give the rows
of celery a thorough soaking through the mulch.
If a special mulch is not used, shallow tillage must
be followed from the time the plants are set until
blanching time.

Provided celery has been started properly and
the plants are healthy and sturdy when finally set
in the permanent rows, the subsequent care is simple. To stimulate growth at first, a little additional nitrate of soda may be scattered along the
row, two or three times, at ten-day intervals. Dis-
solve this salt by a fine spray from the hose, washing it through the mulch and into the soil. Let
the stimulant be given when the plants are to be
watered. That is best done in the cool of the
morning, since cold water is used. As soon as
the surface begins to dry in the yard-wide strip
of bare soil between the mulched rows, tillage
must follow straightway. At the same time pull
the weeds in the mulch and along the row among
the plants. Celery must have plenty of water.
Unless the rainfall is regular and sufficient water
is thus provided, the rows should be thoroughly
soaked at least three times during the period of
greatest growth. As soon as the surface begins
to dry, follow it up with shallow tillage between
the mulch strips. As the plants approach ma-

turity, use water sparingly. Use none at all for several days before blanching.

If the plants are kept growing vigorously, little attention will be needed to protect garden celery from insects or disease. When large fields are grown for the market, fighting disease is often serious; and sometimes insect pests make havoc with the crop. In the home garden, however, a little attention at the proper time will be all that is necessary.

When celery plants are full grown, they must be blanched before they are ready for the table. Blanching is simply depriving them of their color and preventing any further color formation, allowing growth to proceed in the dark. There are several methods suited to the season and the convenience of the gardener. To get early celery ready for the table, only ten to twenty days are required in warm growing weather. Do not blanch too much at once, because the process itself injures the keeping quality. Be sure the plants are dry before they are touched, lest the hearts should rot. Choose a cool clear bright day. At first, a few plants may be tied up in paper to shut out the light. To carry out this simple plan, only ordinary wrapping paper and some twine are needed. Get the gardener's handy paper twine. Run the end through a crochet bag or a little pail hung over the arm. Begin the wrapping of the first plants when they are nearly a foot high.

With a bunch held together by one hand, begin at the bottom and press the stalks close together while the twine is wound about them to the top. Then roll the paper and fasten it tightly around the plant with one edge touching the ground. If necessary, use a second layer to bring the cover clear up to the top. Shove some soil over the edge at the bottom. The plants will continue to grow; and, as they grow, the paper twine stretches and softens and finally breaks. After a time, more paper will be needed to cover the new growth.

This method works well; but it takes more time and the result is no better than when drain-tiles are used. Unglazed tiles are preferable because the unbaked surface provides ventilation. Use four-inch tiles. Merely draw the spreading leaves together and hold them in place with the paper cord, while the tiles are slipped over the top. Push the tile into the soil a bit, hoe the dirt over the bottom and leave the plants to grow white and crisp. Either of these methods brings the quickest results and the product is very good.

Blanching the main part of the early crop with boards is practiced largely in gardens where space is limited. For this plan, procure inch boards, 1 foot wide and about 10 or 12 feet long, suiting the length of the boards somewhat to the amount to be blanched at once. Remember that, after it is deprived of its color of health, the quality soon becomes inferior and there is increasing danger of rot at the heart, especially in sultry midsummer weather. Therefore, start the bleaching of only a part at one time. With the boards laid along the row on each side, set the edges close against the crown, fastening them in place with stout stakes driven into the ground not much farther from the plants than the thickness of the board. Leave just enough room to slip the boards into place. Shove them up close against the foliage, keeping the leaves upright; fasten the top edges with cleats or wire, leaving no more than 2 or 3 inches between; and, last, hoe the soil carefully against the bottom to exclude every bit of light. This method is widely used and the product is excellent celery.

When there is sufficient room, blanching may be done merely with soil. This plan involves more work but it produces the best quality and the finest flavor. With earth blanching, however, there is especial danger of rust at the hearts, if dirt gets in; of rot at the hearts or anywhere else in the plants, if water enters. The plants must be dry when first handled and whenever more soil is added. With dwarf varieties, begin when the celery is 10 inches high; with taller growing sorts, when they are a foot high. Then sturdy healthy plants will measure about a foot across. Gather the bunch of spreading leaves in one hand, while the soil is pressed close to the stems. Do not allow a particle of dirt to get into the hearts. To aid in securing upright growth, the leaves may be kept erect with the paper twine, by running it along the row from plant to plant as each clump is bound close. As the celery grows, more soil must be added. Follow growth with higher broader banks of earth until, finally, barely a fringe of green shows at the top. As soon as the foliage is practically hidden, one end of the bank may be opened. For the care that has been given, the gardener has a right to expect big tender stalks of crisp, white, fine-flavored celery.

Winter celery must be blanched in storage; otherwise it will not keep. Soon after the young plants are set, they may be earthed up enough to start upright growth. Soil may be added once more before cold weather begins. Leave the late crop out as long as possible, for, while severe freezing may impair the flavor, heavy frost cannot hurt sturdy celery growth. Early in November or whenever the weather makes it necessary, the fall celery is put into storage. A part of the late crop may be stored in the house cellar, provided a sufficiently low temperature can be maintained and good ventilation secured. Celery absorbs odors freely; and the flavor will be spoiled if celery is stored with odorant vegetables in an unventilated cellar. Do not pack the plants in a compact mass. Separate the rows by means of boards placed 8 or 10 inches apart; or set them close together in long narrow trench-like boxes. Provide plenty of moist sand or clean garden soil around the roots. As soon as storing is done, the roots should be watered in order to start new growth. Great care will be necessary to prevent black-rot from ruining the crop. Take pains to turn the water merely on the soil, and keep the air fresh and cool. Under these conditions, the new growth produced in the dark cellar will be fine-flavored and almost pure white and exquisitely tender.

While the cellar makes a good celery store-house, under prime conditions, the larger part of the late crop is stored in the garden in trenches. Instead of banking the soil about the plants, however, place the celery below the surface to protect it from the severe cold, while the blanching proceeds. Prepare a trench, 8 to 10 inches wide and as deep as the plants are tall, with plenty of loose soil at the bottom. Force a spading-fork or a garden shovel well below the roots and move the plants, soil-covered roots and all, to the trench. Set them close together, the tops even with the surface. Pack the soil carefully about the roots. Cover the lightly packed row of celery with straw and leaves and corn-stalks, adding more protection as the cold increases. Unless the weather becomes too warm and black-rot attacks the plants, we will find fresh, crisp, white celery, ready for use by the time fresh growing things are most scarce and most needed. The supply in the cellar will last, perhaps, through the holidays; then the garden store may be ready. There will be snow-white tender hearts for a relish, brittle crisp stalks to be cut into salad, or creamed, or used in soup. Whatever remains may be stored in jars before its best flavor is gone. Every bit of the plant, root crown and leaf tops as well as the white crisp stalks, may be used. From the first paper blanched stalks to the last plant in the trench, the celery adds attractiveness to the table and zest to the appetite and renders the food more palatable and healthful.

XIX

SWEET CORN

SWEET CORN needs plenty of room; but even in the city back-yard garden, with economical planning, room may surely be found. Grow it on the garden border. Use its luxuriance as a hedge or as a shelter, placing shade-demanding plants on its shady side. Somehow or other be sure to grow it in the city garden. As for country gardens, there's no question about finding plenty of room for sweet corn. Make a place for pop-corn, also, this ancient close relation of Indian corn. A little pop-corn goes a long way. A small pint cup of the kernels fills an eight-quart pan heaping full of the snowy fragrance.

Expense should be of no account in securing seed; get the best possible, the first season. After that, if the product is satisfactory and suits the taste, we will grow our own seed. Among the endless number of varieties, in choosing, there are two plans to follow. We may choose early and midseason and late varieties and grow them in a succession. For example, put in Golden Bantam (Plate IV) for the early corn; after a few days, plant Country Gentleman; and, again in a few weeks, put in Stowell's Evergreen. Another plan is to choose the very best variety and make successional plantings of this one kind. Suppose, for this first year, we try Golden Bantam. Its quality is excellent: and when ready for the table, its smooth fine-flavored ears are a rich yellow. Growing one variety makes the production of our own seed much simpler and surer. When different varieties are grown in the same garden, the wind is sure to scatter the pollen wide and corn mixes with unusual readiness.

Sweet corn requires a rich sandy loam, well-drained and evenly prepared, for best results. That means merely good garden soil, carefully made ready. If possible, choose an early strip with a southern exposure for the first planting. Do not put in the corn until the soil is thoroughly warm and fairly dry. Sweet corn germinates exceptionally well; every kernel sprouts. Yet the seed is especially liable to rot, if the ground is cold and wet. A little corn might be started in the hotbed, in berry boxes, or in hand-made paper pots. Sometimes this plan of getting an early start is tried with some success; but, usually, transplanting corn does not pay. Corn seedlings are so shallow-rooted that they do not withstand moving. If you decide to try early planting, before the danger of frost is over, put in a few hills in the sunniest spot in the garden. Then cover the seedlings on cold nights with melon boxes or with newspapers laid over the measuring line stretched a little above the row of hills. In planting so early, be sure to provide for the loss by rotting; allow a third more kernels. Always put in more than are needed, even in the late plantings; then the poorest weakest sprouts may be pulled.

There are two methods of planting sweet corn— in rows and in hills. When planting in rows, measure them at least 3 feet apart, and scatter the kernels with 3 or 4 inches between them, in a furrow less than 2 inches deep. After thinning, the plants should stand 12 to 18 inches apart for the dwarf varieties, and nearly 2 feet for the later bigger sorts. For 6 inches in every direction the soil around a healthy plant is crowded full of roots. Provide plenty of room for root growth. At silking time each root should have a cubic foot of space. For big crops of field corn, this method is necessarily used, because in order to save time, a big money factor in corn-raising, these great crops are put in with machinery. Time, however, is no real factor in raising garden corn; and planting sweet corn in rows has real disadvantages. Even when the drilled corn is thinned until it stands nearly 3 feet apart, the light and sunshine do not reach all of the plants equally. Not so much corn can be grown, because in the drilled rows one plant stands alone, while in the rows of hills, the clump may have four plants. The rows

are more difficult to care for; and they are not
nearly so attractive as the regularly arranged hill
clumps of growing corn. Lay off the rows 3 feet
apart; and mark the hills, also, 3 feet apart, ar-
ranging them alternately as though the hills were
at the corners of geometrical diamonds or squares.
That allows for even thorough cultivation between
the parallel rows and diagonally and also about
each hill. Whether planted in hills or in rows, be
sure to scatter the cutworm deterrent, tobacco
waste, beneath the kernels; cover them with at
least an inch of earth in dry weather and then
firm well.

As soon as the green hill clumps are plain to be
seen and the sturdiest shoots of corn show big and
green, the first attention is required. Give the
young corn a stimulating food and with it provide
any food supplement needed for this special vegetable. At the same time, begin to thin the weakest sprouts. Then start cultivation. Plenty of
food for general vegetable growth was placed in
the soil by the fall preparation. An abundance of
natural fertilizers, the reliable food supply for
big corn growth, was plowed under at that time.
However, it requires time for the complete disintegration and the chemical changes necessary to
convert this material into that which produces
growth. Later in the season, as the roots reach
down into the moist lower levels of soil, they will
find these rich food stores prepared to make con-

tinuous lusty growth. Scatter wood-ashes between the rows, twice in the early part of the season; and sprinkle nitrate of soda about the hills.
Care is needed in the use of the nitrate lest this
foliage food should defeat the purpose of the ashes
and, instead of a harvest of ears, our corn strip
should produce a crop of silage. Use the nitrate only twice. As we go along the row, pulling
out some of the weakest shoots, scatter a tablespoonful of sodium nitrate around each hill, working it into the soil with a claw-weeder.

After the nitrate and the ashes have been distributed, then cultivate. At first, tillage must be
shallow, for young corn rootlets feed near the surface. As the roots become stronger and turn
down, extending into the soil, work the hook in
further to encourage deep wide-reaching root
growth. Deep rooting anchors the tops against
the sudden heavy winds that sometimes lay the
corn strip flat on the ground. Working the soil
up over the young surface roots and around the
hills also aids the corn in getting a firm grip in
the soil. Deep rooting reaches the moisture in the
under soil and so affords relief in time of drought.
Deep rooting reaches, at the same time, the fresh
food supplies "unlocked" in midsummer. Vary
the depth of tillage to fit root growth; always finish with light stirring of the surface to form the
dust mulch so essential to conserve the moisture

VI.—Head Lettuce, One of the Prizes of the Real Garden.

for steady vigorous development. Cultivate every
ten days or so.

As growth proceeds, pull more of the weakest
shoots until, when about a foot high, four nearly
equally distant sturdy plants remain. When cultivating, watch for the suckers that steal the harvest. With a quick jerk, pull them before they
are fairly started. Be sure these branches do
come from the lowest node, not from the axil of
the first leaf. Sometimes the first true leaf is so
close to the ground that the young ear can scarcely
be distinguished from a sucker until the silk appears. Make certain which is which; and then,
so long as these useless shoots appear, keep them
pulled.

When picking corn be sure to mark the very
biggest, fullest, smoothest ears, one on a stalk, for
seed; and mark more than double the amount
needed. When gathering for the table, do not
slit the husk open to see whether the ear is
ready, as that spoils the ear. Gather early in
the morning while the dew lies fresh and cool
upon the husks. The sugar-content is lost rapidly
after being pulled and stripped. Therefore, leave
them in a cool cellar until nearly dinner time.
Strip the husks then and brush away the silk;
and put the ears into the boiling pot. When grown
properly and gathered at the right time, it does
not matter how fresh sweet corn is cooked. The

first few messes must be cooked and eaten from
the cob.   There is no better way for the corn epi-
cure to taste and test its juiciness and fine flavor.
After a little, when the limas are ready, succotash
may be made instead.   Soufflé or country corn
pudding is excellent for supper.   However prepared, the sweet corn is always a table delight.

We shall expect the crop to be bountiful, even
beyond our hope; far more than we shall be able
to use fresh.   Dry some of the surplus, using the
over-mature ears, especially.   Shave it from the
cobs; spread it on trays in the sunshine or above
the kitchen stove.   Be sure to can the best of the
surplus.   Canned corn may be exactly as delicious
as fresh if it is put up in the best way.   Gather
the corn to be canned very early in the cool of
the morning.   Strip the husks and remove the silk
immediately; and then put it into the jars and
begin sterilization.   With a very sharp knife
barely shave the surface of the kernels, cutting
from the stem end towards the ear tip.   Clip the
surface just enough to open the kernel.   Using a
dull knife or the back of the other, scrape out the
heart of the kernel; it is not the hard outside, but
the juicy milky heart of the corn that we wish to
preserve.   Fill the jars partly full, up to the
curve near the top; no fuller, otherwise, when the
jars are heated and the corn expands, the very
juiciest part, the milk, runs over and is wasted.
It might be well to slip the ears into boiling water

to set the milk. Leave plenty of room in the jars for expansion. Snap the wire down or screw on the top tight. Then no corn is wasted, no flavor lost. Whether ordinary sap buckets with home-devised false-bottoms and lids are used and the old unvaryingly reliable three-day process followed, or whether a pressure canner is employed is immaterial in the quality of the product.

Looking toward the next year's harvest means caring for the seed. The best of the crop was chosen for seed; and enough ears were marked to allow for rigid selection. Leave the seed corn ungathered until the husks and stalks are withered and dry. Then, we may be sure that the fullest development has been reached. Now, break off the ears and strip the husks down, leaving a few attached to the ear so that we may braid the corn. When the braiding is finished, then we will hang up the golden corn in the old-fashioned way, along the garret rafters or in some other cool dry place to "cure" or season. After the ears are thoroughly hard and dry, make the final selection of the choicest ones,—ears that are long and uniform and full-kernelled to the tip. Run the hand down these chosen ears to make sure they are smooth and evenly filled. A braid of such ears ought to bring the best prize at the Fair. Finally, our "selected seed corn" must be stored for winter. Make sure that the agencies that induce or aid germination are absent. Moisture and warmth together will spoil the seed, just because, as we have already found, their united action produces germination. Seeds like corn, containing a good deal of moisture, cannot so well endure either a very high or a low temperature.

The drier the seeds, the greater the variation of temperature they can endure. Shell the seed corn and store it in paper bags or boxes in a cool dry room.

XX

CRESS

IF spring water is accessible, an abundant supply of this stimulating salad plant may be grown, even enough for the neighborhood, with no trouble but the sowing of the seed. This persistent perennial, once given a start, grows on forever so long as the water from the spring continues to flow. Along the border of the garden that has yielded such rich and varied returns is a narrow open stream, the overflow from the home spring. It lies at the foot of the orchard slope where the flickers call, an ever-living exhaustless spring, with its source deep back in the hillside above. The bank of this spring ditch is a part of the perennial strip of the garden. On the moist banks and in the wet grass at the mouth of the spring, the water-cress thrives. Every spring, long before the last snow and ice are gone from the hillside, its fresh green marks the course of the open stream. The peppermint also grows near the spring; and, when its pungent fragrance comes from the wet grass, the water-cress is at its best, its fresh crisp shoots spicy and appetizing and enticing. Bread and butter and water-cress salad

141

are supper enough, any day in the early spring. Tired with the monotony of the winter fare, the peppery water-cress refreshes and stimulates the appetite and leaves a new hungry taste. Once started, this spring relish cares entirely for itself. Among the wet grasses around the spring, along the damp border of the little stream, wherever the water from the spring works its way, the water-cress spreads its spicy green.

If you do not own a spring, you may possibly have a real brook running through the pasture hills. Scatter the seeds in the wet rich soil near the running water and find the cress ready for the picnic supper that you are sure to have often by the side of the cool shady brook. For growing water-cress, the neighbor's brook is yours; but be certain that the water is pure.

Perhaps you have no spring; and no brook can be found. Then we will merely do our best with the garden variety or pepper-grass. Some kinds of this common garden cress, like "Extra Curled," have beautifully curled foliage with rich compact growth. When started in the early spring in a moist shady place, kept fresh and crisp with plenty of water, and gathered while young and tender, pepper-grass does very well. Garden cress keeps tender and fresh only a few days. Gather it all before any sign of the flower-buds appear. Pepper-grass might surely be given a place in the city garden, under the cherry-tree shade, in the deep rich soil, next the old barn. Sow it very early; and keep it very wet with water from the hose. Grow it in window-boxes in the garret or in a sunny window, down cellar; and have a winter taste of this biting green appetizer.

XXI

CUCUMBERS; ALSO PUMPKINS, MELONS AND SQUASHES

Good results may be secured with cucumbers on clay or loam or sandy soils. Because of the dangers from extremes of temperature, however, the season in our northern gardens is necessarily short for this sensitive plant. The soil must be of such make and tilth that a quick start is assured. While clay loams or more retentive heavier soils serve well for later plants, a warm sandy loam properly prepared is necessary for the earlier plantings. Whatever the soil, it must have the proper preparation. In fitting the cucumber strip, special foresight is needed with reference to moisture conservation. Both the vines and the fruit are unusually succulent, and must have an abundance of water for healthy steady growth. Much can be done to make the most of the soil supply of water, through careful tillage and by the use of abundance of humus in the hills. If the soil-moisture is wasted by careless preparation, the injury to growth at the start can never be repaired. The harvest is largely lost at the outset. Proper tillage produces an even distribu-

144

tion of the moisture and the humus holds it in
readiness for use. The soil must also be warm;
a cold soil is a fatal shock to the vitality of cucumbers. Moreover, there must be plenty of food
at hand entirely ready for use. Nothing must
be allowed to hinder growth. With early warm
soil properly fitted and supplied with plenty of
the necessary food, a quick start may be expected
and growth should be immediate and steady and
healthy.

Much may be accomplished at the outset by the
method of starting the young cucumber plants.
The real growing season may be lengthened
merely by sprouting the seeds or by starting the
plants in a warm place. Cucumbers transplant
with difficulty. Like corn and beans, they have
but few fibrous roots, and their single sprout-root
is brittle and easily broken. Even so, if the
proper material is used in seeding, these delicate
plants may be transplanted readily and safely.
In our short northern season everything possible
must be done to secure an early start, especially
with varieties that must ripen. The old-fashioned
warm place under the kitchen stove will do very
well for sprouting the seeds on inverted sods;
but the hotbed is better. There considerable
growth may be made before transplanting.
Cucumbers may be started in the warmth of the
hotbed nearly a month before the outdoor garden
is warm enough. Use shallow breakable sods or

moss placed in paper pots or berry boxes, any
material that may be transplanted together with
the delicate seedlings. Dampen the sods or moss,
sprinkle fine soil over their root surfaces; then
scatter the seeds between, plenty to allow for all
loss, say four times as many as needed for the
crop. With such a start, cucumbers may be ready
for salad two or three weeks earlier and the gardener may be much surer of ripe fruit. As soon
as the ground is warm enough, usually early in
June, plantings may be made in the open.

Whether sown in the open garden or transplanted from the hotbed, cucumbers are always
grown in hills. Lay out the hills at least 4 feet
apart and spade them deeply 2 feet across, making
the soil even and fine and loose. At the bottom
of the hills, well below the young roots, put some
thoroughly rotted manure or compost material
to lighten the soil and at the same time hold the
moisture. Add to that a shovelful of the heat-
producing stimulating hen-manure or a little
commercial fertilizer. Cover it all with soil to
protect the roots from burning. On top of this
layer of soil scatter the seeds or arrange the
pieces of sod with the small plants from the hotbed, taking care not to injure the frail tap-roots.
Put them 2 inches apart and be sure to allow for
all dangers from frost and beetles and disease.
If a quarter of the seeds or even the plants survive the difficulties and dangers of early life, we

shall be satisfied. For every hill, the careful gardener may fairly expect three or four healthy sturdy plants.

Everything possible must be done to bring about immediate vigorous growth and continuous development. With all vegetables a quick start means food and moisture and tillage. With vines, especially, food that is completely ready for assimilation is absolutely necessary. The ammonia in the hen-manure at the bottom of the hills will produce steady growth, once the roots can reach this rich supply. In the meantime, a little nitrate about the hills will aid in getting growth started. Use it often, once a fortnight until midsummer, for the salad cucumbers. With those grown for hard little pickles and the big ones for ripe fruit when firm texture is so necessary, discontinue the nitrate as soon as growth has started. After that, if anything further is used, let it be, instead, a scattering of wood-ashes.

For the season's supply of moisture so essential to the succulent cucumbers, much was done in the general soil preparation and in the special fitting of the cucumber strip at planting time. Providing moisture-holding material and securing a light loose condition of the soil has already placed in readiness the entire supply of water. As we know, continual surface tillage will prevent any waste of this natural source of moisture. It may not be sufficient, however; cucumbers—

all vines—are thirsty plants; they must have
abundance of water. If it becomes necessary to
supplement the supply in the soil, use water that
has become somewhat warm by standing. The
cold water from the hose, even when turned on
the ground in the morning, shocks the vitality of
these warm-season vines. Water the cucumbers
towards night; pour the stream of water into the
center of the hill and down each stem. The importance of thorough work in artificial watering
cannot be over-emphasized. Give each hill all the
water it will absorb. Soak the soil clear through
to the moist lower layers and in the morning stir
the surface to prevent any waste through evaporation. A sufficient water supply is certainly
indispensable; but most important to immediate,
steady, vigorous growth is tillage. From planting
time until the vines completely shade the surface,
tillage must be maintained. If early tillage is
neglected, subsequent attention cannot repair the
damage. The stunted wizened growth can never
be changed into vigorous fruit-bearing vines. The
best surface tillage is necessary to get the plants
so well established in vigorous growth that plenty
of blossoms set before the blighting heat of midsummer.

With all vines, while intelligent care is bring-
ing about vigor, much may be accomplished
toward fruit production by the control of growth.

As soon as the plants are three or four inches high or whenever danger from disease or insects is over, if too many are left, the poorest may be pulled. At blossoming time, we hope the vines will have vigor enough so that several fruits may set at once. Do not allow the energy of the vine to be so expended, so usurped in the development of a first fruit that later ones are smaller and imperfect in development. Unless a single cucumber is being grown for a special purpose, as for exhibit, snip off the first ones until several set at once. In this way, we may to some extent control fruit production. To gain the result desired, it may be necessary also to control vine growth. Too luxuriant growth of vine is usually at the expense of the harvest of fruit. In that case, if the vines grow big and long and the cucumbers do not set or, after setting, they do not develop well, pinch the ends of the vines. In growing ripe cucumbers, it is especially necessary to control growth and also not allow fruit to continue to set too late in the season to mature. Controlling vine growth and fruit setting will aid much in improving quality and hastening maturity. Cucumbers are also a prey to disease and insect enemies, to an unusual degree. Beetles may be disposed of by hand-picking or they may be kept away by covering the young plants, by dusting with poison, or by arsenical poison sprays. Spray with "black

leaf 40" tobacco extract for plant-lice. Spraying
with bordeaux mixture is effective against cucumber diseases.

Every garden must make room for cucumbers,
even in the city. The average kind of soil, if it
is in the best possible condition, will give good
results. The best English cucumbers are always
grown in the limited space of the forcing-house.
We might try growing them along the line fence
or on a wire trellis over the old barn. Get seeds
of the Japanese climbing variety. Like the wild
cucumber vine, let this climbing variety cover
some unsightly place with beauty and fragrance
and at the same time provide fresh cool salad.
Be sure of plenty of sunlight. The Japanese cucumber is especially adapted to dry weather.
Give the plants every care at first. Start them
just like any cucumber. Feed them nitrate until
vigorous growth is assured. When they begin
to climb, stir some mixed fertilizer into the soil
about the hills. Give them continual surface
tillage and protect them from their foes, and even
in the limited space so precious to the city folks,
cucumbers may richly pay. There is plenty of
room, of course, in the country garden. The garden vines should all be grown near by, in one wide
strip at the side of the garden. Then the running
vines will be out of the way. They may be used
as a companion crop with various other vegetables.
Any plant that matures before the vines need

the space between the rows may be very frugally grown in the cucumber patch. Lettuce would do well or early beets. Bush beans are an excellent companion for cucumbers in more ways than one. The rapid upright growth of the beans serves as a protection to the young cucumber plants. They furnish a good lure for their worst enemy; they are out of the way before the area is needed; the ground is left better than they found it, for beans will leave in the soil a new supply of food for the hungry cucumbers. Beans seem to be the best companion crop; but tuck in anything rather than leave the ground between the vine rows unutilized.

For varieties, White Spine is good for a refreshing salad; Cool and Crisp is an excellent variety both for slicing and for the tiny pickles or, if you are planning for a quantity of little pickles, get the Burr cucumber, used only for pickling. For the old-fashioned big sweet yellow pickles, nothing takes the place of Long Green. If only one variety is to be grown, then you must choose Everbearing, which grows all sorts of fruit well, from the tiny size used for pickles to the big ones allowed to mature. It keeps on blossoming and producing and maturing fruit until frost.

With cucumbers the harvest is continual, from the surprise of the first salad cucumber found beneath the cool sheltering leaves, until the last huge golden fruit is brought to light by the wither-

ing touch of the frost on the cover of leaves.
Care is needed in picking the cucumbers. If
pulled, the whole plant is liable to be loosened at
the root. Cut the fruit, instead, with a knife or
the garden shears, leaving a bit of the stem on
the main stalk. The cucumbers must be gathered
as fast as they are ready, the Burrs when less
than two inches. Gather them all. Never let
fruit ripen on vines growing salad; new fruit will
not continue to form, as a rule, while more developed fruit is ripening. The ripening process,
the development of seed, is a great strain on the
plant vitality. If fruit is allowed to mature, productive vigor will be wasted; so, unless the
gardener wishes merely ripe fruit, as with the
Long Green, keep the fruit all harvested as soon
as the desired size is reached. By care in harvesting at the proper time, the harvest is pro-
longed and the quality improved. Look the vines
over every day or two. Cut in the morning, while
it is cool, for the refreshing flavor lies in the cool
juice and the crisp texture.

No one needs telling how to use cucumbers:
for salad, whether sliced into a French dressing
or served with vinegar or merely a shake of salt.
Try tarragon vinegar in the French dressing.
Pare them and chop them a bit and, added to any
salad, they furnish the cool, refreshing, fragrant
quality like no other salad fruit. Pile the slices
on lettuce leaves and dress them merely with salt.

The simplest way of serving salad cucumbers is the most satisfying. There are various ways to preserve them for winter. Make jars and jars of the little pickles; don't miss having some sweet chunk pickles made of the bigger fruit. Save every ripe cucumber for the unrivaled old-fashioned sweet pickle. One can never have too much mustard pickle put away for the time when the dull appetite needs sharpening.

Pumpkins

Nearly all that has been said concerning growing cucumbers is true with the culture of all the vines. The knowledge necessary to raise a crop of cucumbers, the most sensitive and delicate, the most difficult, of all the cucurbits, is more than sufficient for growing melons, pumpkins and squashes.

The big field pumpkins, even though they may be had for the taking, are not the best sort. They are exactly right for Hallowe'en Jack-o'-lanterns. They may be made most terrifying with their witch-like cavernous grin appearing suddenly out of the darkness against the window pane on a weird November night; and as suddenly disappearing with a scamper of feet across the porch; and again to be seen down in the dark corn field at the opening of the corn-shock wigwam. They are good for fun at bonfires. These huge pumpkins are all right for anything except for pumpkin pies. Instead, choose one of the varieties developed especially for pies. Where these little pie pumpkins are grown does not much matter. The seeds might be planted with the sweet corn if the corn strip is near the garden border, so that the vines can be turned aside into the grass out of the way. They have little disease and do not seem to be bothered with the enemies so dangerous to some of their vine relations. Just put in the seeds, somewhere, and they are bound to grow. At the corn harvest, you will always find plenty.

Melons

Watermelons and muskmelons need a sunny sandy shallow hollow on the hillslope. Of course in our northern climate, the season is so short that raising watermelons is a real venture; but it is surely worth trying and it has been done successfully. Growing the huge fruits is much the same in soil culture and care as for cucumbers. The question of food is a little different. Do not give the watermelons any nitrogen compound. Feed them, instead, an abundance of potash-containing fertilizers. It is said that much nitrogen will injure the delicate sweetness of the watermelon flavor. With all the kinds of muskmelons, sweetness and flavor are not apparently so dependent on the correct selection of fertilizer. These luscious fruits are not so dependent, either,

on climate.   Perfect harvests are produced as far
north as Canada.   There are, however, certain so-
called special melon centers throughout the
country.   Unless the soil is heavy and low, the
home garden might possibly prove to be a real
melon center.   Try a few bush melons in the
garden; and plant others on the watermelon plan-
tation.   All these melons need more room than
the cucumbers, but the same intelligent care that
is given the sensitive cucumber ought to produce
plenty of delicious fruit ready for use in the early
fall.   We should surely want to try, sometime,
the joyous adventure of growing melons.

Among watermelons, there are early small-
fruited sweet varieties that mature in the short
seasons of northern gardens.   Give them a warm
place and light "quick" soil.   The watermelons
(Plate V) are handsome fruits to grow.

Squashes

When it comes to squashes, there is no question
about making room for them in the country garden.   Our city garden plot, also, may find space
for even the big lusty-growing winter squash.   A
friend who lives in the heart of a little city in a
section where space is so valuable for churches
and schools that there is scarce room for a rose-
garden, grew Hubbard squashes successfully.
Rather, the squashes grew themselves.   Some
seeds had been scattered by chance on the bare

area of the winter ash-pile and lean coal-ashes. The seeds sprouted and started to grow. In the fall the vagrant uncared-for seedling produced a most real harvest. The vines ran along in the grass close by the house and, having made strong permanent growth, they actually climbed the eaves' spout in a sheltering angle of the house; and, there, beneath the cornice in the bend of the eaves' pipe, was a Boston Marrow squash, almost ripe.

Some practical suggestions may be of value in growing winter squashes in the roomy country garden. Placed on the garden border, the big vines will have plenty of room to spread themselves; and the grass will protect the squashes from midsummer heat and from the beetles. Unless disposed of permanently, the persistent beetles will be on hand, in the fall, and they may ruin our cherished Hubbard squashes. To keep well, the shells must be hard; and to be fine of flavor and mealy, the squashes must not be watery. Feed the young plants plenty of potash and you may be sure of fine-flavored, firm-textured, hard-shelled squashes. Pruning squashes is of special importance. A few thoroughly developed well-ripened squashes are much more satisfactory in the end than a host of half-developed fruit. Allow only a few squashes to set on each vine. Pinch off all the others and also pinch the vine-ends as soon as enough fruit has begun to develop.

The winter squash has enemies apparently peculiar to itself. The rusty-black squash stink-bug lays its eggs on the under sides of the leaves of the young plants. The nymphs that hatch from the smooth shining brown eggs feed on the life of the plants, sucking the sap and greatly injuring the plant health. Of course the netting-covered boxes will furnish protection; but watch out for this enemy. Look for the eggs and destroy them. If the eggs escape our search, the tobacco spray used for the aphids, which also attack squashes sometimes, may dispose of these parasites as well.

Nothing must be allowed to endanger the harvest of winter squashes. The delicious mealy golden squash must have its place on the Thanksgiving table. It is indispensable for the Christmas dinner. To be sure of prime squash for midwinter, the fruit must be stored exactly right or canned when quality and texture are best. Storing squashes is especially important. Do not put them under cover too early. Leave them on the big vines to continue maturing, until the vines have died or until frost has burned them. When the cold nights threaten, old bagging may be thrown over the squashes. Protect them in some way from the increasing cold; but leaving the squashes out hardens them and improves the quality. After the time comes for cleaning the garden, the squashes may be cut and stacked on the garden border. Cut with a piece of the vine

stalk left attached to the big fruit to prevent rotting at the stem.   Gather and pile carefully to
guard against injury.   Finally, when nearly
freezing weather has come, they should be taken
indoors.   Even then they must be kept in a cool
dry place just above freezing.   When properly
harvested and stored, Warted Hubbard will keep
well.   Warmth and dampness are sure to induce
rot.   As soon as the hard shells show the first
sign of rot, the squashes should be stored in glass
jars.

Even when at their best quality, at least a
part of the crop should be canned.   Winter
squash is especially satisfactory canned.   The
fresh flavor and texture keep for several years
and, by storing in jars, there is none of the trouble
of handling and caring for in storage; no danger
of loss; and, best of all, at a minute's notice, there
is squash for dinner, for those incomparable
squash biscuits, and for pies that are better
flavored, richer, than even the long-famed pumpkin pies.   To serve fresh, squash is especially good
baked.   The centers may be removed and mashed,
seasoned, and made deliciously tender with cream
and served directly from the shells.

It will be easy to grow summer squashes.   Some
like the long melon-like Delicata, the between-
seasons squash that is at its best just after the
frost has finished the summer squashes.   The
Patty-Pan, a creamy-white, scalloped and some-

what flattened squash, is considered excellent.
To my taste, however, there is no early variety
like the luscious tender Golden Crookneck.
Treat these summer squashes much like salad cucumbers. Feed the young plants plenty of nitrate
of soda and they will grow big and really beautiful, and the fruit will then be very tender and delicate and fine of flavor. The sturdy crooknecks do
not need the careful attention that must be given
the sensitive cucumber. Their lusty growth is,
usually, perfectly healthy, almost never a prey
to disease. Insect enemies do not trouble them
much; the beetles do not seem to fancy the big
leaves.

Summer squashes are very prolific. Only a few
hills will be needed; give them plenty of room and
allow only two or three plants to a hill. Give
them ordinary care and, very soon, the big yellow
blossoms will begin to appear and, soon afterwards, the little crooknecks. None should be
allowed to ripen, unless one plant is to provide
seed. Gather all the fruits when they are just
exactly right. That is before the shell is hard,
while the thumb still pierces the surface easily,
and brings a spurt of the juice. If they are too
small, they will be flavorless. If the fruit is all
gathered when ready, these lusty plants will continue to produce the little crooknecks even until
the first frost that burns and withers the mammoth sheltering leaves. Keep a lookout beneath

the leaves.   Cut all the fruit as soon as it is ready.
Gather it early and keep cool until time to get
dinner.   Then steam and mash, tender shells, seeds
and all, and season with salt and pepper and
serve hot.   Their own flavor is condiment enough.
Summer squash is very satisfactory canned.
When used the first winter, their fresh flavor is
retained.

XXII

LETTUCE; ALSO ENDIVE, WITLOOF AND CORN-SALAD

WITH no variety of vegetable is the result more dependent on the special kind of seed than with lettuce. The proper care and food will change the flavor and texture, almost the very nature of many vegetables. Plenty of potash fertilizer will produce firm-textured, thick-meated, golden sweet-pickle cucumbers out of the succulent salad fruit. Excluding the sunlight changes the tough acrid green celery to a fine-flavored, brittle-textured, white appetizer. To produce head lettuce of fine quality the gardener must sow head lettuce seed. Head lettuce (Plate VI) is one of the prizes of the garden.

Varieties should be chosen with reference to the season. Any loose-leaved quick-growing lettuce is especially suited to the early spring. Curly-leaved or some other early sort like Grand Rapids may be started in window-boxes or in the hotbed. Frost does not kill lettuce, and for that reason the first sowing may be made in the open ground; but growth is sure to be slow in the cold weather of early spring; and slow growth

161

produces tough texture and bitter flavor. Therefore, the fortunate possessor of a hotbed will grow the first lettuce in its sheltering warmth. When the air and the soil outside are warm enough, the young lettuce plants may be removed to the garden; but, if there is room, they are much better matured where they have begun to make tender growth. As the leaves become large enough, they are picked; and, so long as the new growth is tender and the flavor still delicate, or until the seed-stalks begin to form, the leaves may still be gathered. The same old-fashioned plan is followed with the early garden lettuce bed sometimes. In the old gardens, the lettuce seed was scattered broadcast over a broad bed, hoed up or ridged high enough to provide surface drainage and to secure air and warmth of the spring sunshine throughout the bed. Scattered thickly over the surface, the seed was raked in. Then, as the plants developed, the biggest leaves were gathered until the plants began to go to seed. The loose-leaved lettuces are satisfactory for the hotbed; but I should choose some variety of head lettuce for even the first outdoor sowing.

Mignonette lettuce was discovered in a hunt through the catalogue for something new. The name was attraction enough to make sure of a trial. The seeds were sown by chance among the young summer squash plants; and, as the little heads of Mignonette lettuce began to form, they were shaded from the hot flavor-embittering sunshine by the great wide-spreading squash leaves. They were almost forgotten. On looking for the first crooknecks, there, in the cool shade of the big plants, were the little brown heads in a tight-packed row. The extra nitrogen-providing food that made the yellow squashes cool-tasting and tender and succulent, made the lettuce crispy and delicate beyond description. When gathered in the cool of the early morning, one of the tiny brown heads with the creamy-white heart laid open on the plate was just salad enough for one. This delicate lettuce may be grown all summer, thus sheltered in some way.

Another variety especially fine for fall and early winter is Big Boston. One season the gardener came across a package of those seeds. They were sown in a spare plot at midsummer. Not much attention was given the young plants; but here and there in the thickly sown row, heads began to form. As the plants were thinned, the heads grew big and firm. Even after frost had come, these carelessly sown seeds had become a compact growth of big firm heads. There were more than we could use. It seemed too bad to leave them to die. So, as a venture, a kind of coldframe was built about them; the soil was hoed up over the bottom of the frame and an old sash was laid over the top. Now and then a head was removed; and, until nearly Christmas, beneath the snow-

drifted frame, the most delicious tender white-
hearted heads of lettuce were ready for the
freshest spring salad.

There are some other varieties worth considering; and we would do best to choose with care.
Salamander lettuce is rightly named; it produces
crisp fine-flavored heads in spite of hot midsummer weather. The Cos lettuces are also suited
to hot weather. They are a kind of celery lettuce
that form longish heads, blanching mild and crisp,
in spite of the burning heat that tends to embitter
the flavor of any salad plants. With lettuce,
there is a variety for each season, a special kind
for almost every variation of climate. Choosing
the variety to fit the season, lettuce will furnish
fresh salad almost the year around.

While lettuce grows almost anywhere, under
almost any conditions, it needs, for best growth,
a rich sandy loam, well-drained. For early seeding, ridging insures better surface drainage and
more warmth and, therefore, more rapid growth.
An extra supply of nitrogen furnished any salad
plant makes luxuriant crisp growth. Nitrogen-
grown lettuce is so tender that the weight of the
water will actually break the thick buttery leaves
as they are lifted out of the cool cleansing plunge.

While we feed the growing lettuce properly, we
should not forget that any succulent plant is sure
to be thirsty. Give the rows of lettuce plenty of
water, whenever it is really needed. Let the sur-

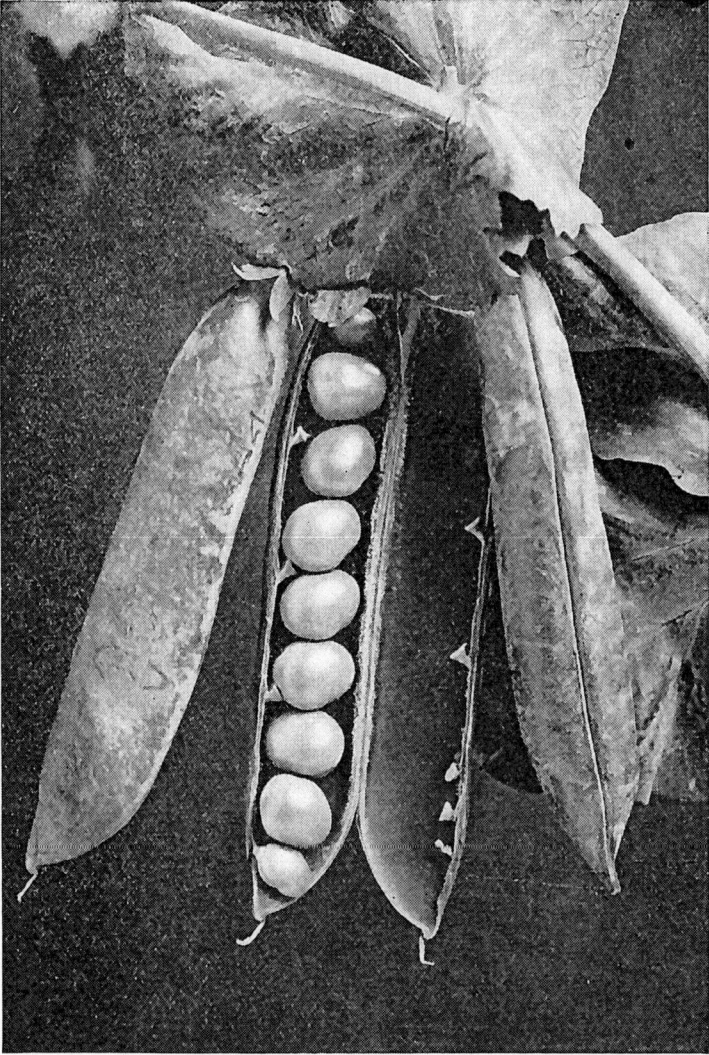

VII.—Garden Peas.—"Not one pod need be wasted."

face become dry, however, before watering, else
we shall find that lettuce has disease to fight.
Sometimes, when the soil is poorly drained or is
kept too wet, and also when surface tillage is neglected, the leaves begin to soften or rot where
they touch the ground. This rhizoctonia or
bottom-rot is often very destructive where large
quantities of lettuce are grown for market. A
slimy rot sometimes appears in muggy midsummer weather. In the home garden, however, there
need be no difficulty from any disease. Be careful
about the watering. Sometimes, small garden
snails will herd on the lettuce, especially if the
surface is left untilled; and sometimes the
aphids will prove a nuisance. A good hard hosing, in the early morning, will drive off these
garden leeches, and water the plants at the same
time. Stirring the soil often will keep them away.
Furnish plenty of clear air about the plants and
in the surface soil by thorough thinning and careful shallow cultivation. Lettuce thus grown in
well-drained, well-aërated, sandy soil, well-fed and
carefully tended, will be sure to be healthy and
thrifty.

Somewhere in the garden, there is always just
the right sheltered spot for the lettuce. Be sure
to have a little growing somewhere, all the season
through, for this salad plant is needed, in some
form, every day. Early in the season, lettuce
alone is most satisfying. For the spring lettuce

salad, no carefully combined dressing—whether French dressing at its best or the smoothest mayonnaise—can take the place of a shake of salt and a sprinkle of sugar and, then, plenty of rich country cream. Gather the lettuce early while moist with the cool dew; clean it and freshen the hearts with plenty of cold water. Then put it aside in the cheese-cloth bag near the ice, ready for the whole day's need.

The endives are well worth growing both for blanching for hot weather salad and also for winter salads. They make a beautiful garnish and their rather acrid flavor is excellent for soups and stews. When grown for winter use, they may be protected outside in mild climates or stored indoors, like celery. They form large hearts when blanched; and furnish a delicious winter salad.

Witloof chicory, the "Barbe de Capucin" of the French, is a winter joy to the salad lover. Grown to maturity out-of-doors, the roots are then replanted in soil in the cellar. The quickly sprouting, fresh, crisp growth of this winter lettuce is most appetizing in the scarce winter-time.

Corn-salad or "Lamb's lettuce" is another variety that has a place of its own in the garden. Sow the seeds of these hardy little plants in the fall; and, when spring comes, find them fresh and green, ready for use.

XXIII

ONIONS AND CHIVES

THERE are several sorts of onions: the top onions that do not form like an ordinary bulb but are produced on the flower-stalk in the place of real blossoms; the multiplier onions which have more than one heart; and sets which are merely partially developed onions. Early spring onions may be grown from seed, but to save time they are usually developed from these sets. The sets are grown the summer before and are started from seeds. The seed is scattered so closely and so near the surface that through over-crowding and from lack of food and moisture, growth is arrested while the bulbs are small. The tops soon die and the tiny onions are ready to be cured and stored. The partial growth of the onions makes them ready for quick development in the early spring. The multiplier or potato onions are also good for early tops for each heart produces a separate bunch of fresh stalks. The top onions or bulblets are also good for early planting. All of these unusual sorts of onions are satisfactory for quick growth of fresh tops and crisp, appetizing bulbs for early salad.

167

For the main-season crop which provides for the fall and the long winter supply, slower firmer development is essential. Whether the variety is the big white luscious Bermuda or the little every-day brown garden onion, they are grown from seed. With the quicker-growing southern varie-ties, the seed may be sown in the hotbed and the seedlings transplanted to the open ground when the weather is warm enough. This furnishes the northern-grown Spanish onions, ready for early fall market. The northern varieties are merely sown in the open garden where they are to mature.

For onions the soil must be fine and free from stones and the surface clear of clods and even and smooth; it should be made just as even and fine of texture as far below the surface as the onions go. The best onion soil is also naturally rich and moist. Keep the surface from packing and do not allow it to dry out and harden; keep it open and loose of texture. Provide plenty of fertilizer near the surface where the onions forage most. Quickly available fertilizer is not especially needed, because the main crop of onions is a long-season one, but it should be placed near at hand. A dressing of wood-ashes to increase the supply of potash and phosphoric acid will be an advan-tage together with a little nitrogenous food to start the delicate seedlings.

The onion crop depends so much on the seed, and this is so variable, that the greatest care is needed in its selection. Pay a good price and secure the best seed. Germination is slow; so scatter the seeds thickly along the smooth-surfaced straight rows, using some quickly germinating seed to mark the rows. Place the rows a foot or more apart. Careful attention must be given to weeding and keeping the top soil stirred. For a successful crop, the onion strip must grow nothing except onions. Sometimes, if the onions have too much foliage food, the tops will grow at the expense of the bulbs. If so, the tops should be broken down by drawing a hoe handle down the garden row or rolling a barrel over.

When the tops begin to wither and dry and harvest time has come, choose a clear dry day for digging. Leave them in rows on the surface to dry and cure for a few days. Cut the tops a half inch above the bulbs. When thoroughly dry, they are ready for storing. Onions ordinarily will not stand freezing and thawing, so they must be stored in a dry frost-proof place. Cared for properly, they will be ready all winter for seasoning and salad, to smother the steak, to serve all tender and white and delicious in cream, or sliced thin with a sprinkle of salt or a spreading of mayonnaise for the salad.

Chives

The delicate onion flavor of chives was formerly esteemed in all kinds of old-fashioned cookery. A

plateful of the quick-growing tender tops is better than young onions with bread and butter.
Chop the fresh shoots and use them to flavor the
soup or the stew, to add snap to the plain sandwich, to give character to salad. Merely secure a
root, which means a bunch of the tiniest onion
bulbs; tuck them in somewhere; and leave them to
grow themselves. If a little care is given the
chives and they are kept cut and watered, their
early mild flavor and tenderness will remain
throughout the season.

XXIV

PARSLEY

WE gardeners may not find time or room, at first, for a regular herb-bed. There will always be hop-vines over a fence, somewhere; catnip in the corner, peppermint in the moist grass near the spring ditch; and spearmint there too for mint sauce. Caraway will look after itself, for it seems suited to an abandoned place. Sage, once started, will care for itself fairly well. Some of these old-time herbs may be depended on to find their own place and make healthy growth, ready for picking. Nearly all do better with care, however.

The time for an old-fashioned herb-bed is sure to come. Then, in addition to some of the wild or vagrant growing herbs, there will be lavender for its sweet smelling old-time evoking perfume; tarragon for the vinegar that makes the best flavored salad dressing; summer savory and fennel and rosemary. Meanwhile we shall need to make room for parsley, the herb that is used most for seasoning soups and sauces and meats; in salad; and as garnish for all sorts of fine cookery. No garden can fully supply the kitchen without this piquant relish. Once started, this sturdy herb will also look after itself. If the grass and weeds are kept out of the parsley plot, it will sow its own seed and keep on growing, year after year. Like all its family, the oily seeds are slow to germinate. Soak them in warm water, over night, and sow them in moist rich soil in a somewhat shady spot. Look after the weeds until sturdy growth is well started. Then you may forget the parsley patch, until some of its rich feathery green is needed. It may be made a year-around plant by sowing the seed in the empty hotbed or in window-boxes in the garret or down cellar. Outdoors, if the snow is heavy enough for protection, just by pushing away the snow, you may find it fresh and green the whole winter through.

XXV

PARSNIPS AND SALSIFY

THESE two roots may well be considered together. Their habits of growth are nearly alike; their culture and care will be much the same. Both parsnips and salsify have long unvarying tapering roots, when grown under proper conditions; and both require an entire season for full development. For firm-textured crisp root growth, there must be provided proper food and a sufficient supply for the entire season. For smooth well-formed roots, the soil must be deep and fine and uniform in texture, free from lumps and stones that impede growth and make crooked branched roots, a difficulty especially liable with salsify. For all plants that have deep growing root systems, the lower soil levels must be well aërated; and a sufficient and continuous moisture supply provided. The careful preparation given our garden in the making has taken into consideration all of these requisites for the production of perfect roots. Good drainage in the very building of the garden, together with the humus incorporated in the soil in the fall preparation, has already provided for soil aëration and a uniform

173

distribution of the supply of water. The well-rotted manure plowed under at that time will be the source of the midsummer food supply. The thorough spring preparation of the soil and the extra commercial fertilizer distributed then will assure a uniform soil texture and provide quickly available food to start growth. Everything seems already to have been provided for the production of a big perfect harvest of parsnips and salsify.

Certain things need attention at planting time. The root strip has been placed on the border near the perennials. The most convenient spot for these long-seasoned roots will be next to the asparagus. There they will be out of the way of the fall plowing and may be left undisturbed through the winter. Experience has convinced the gardener that not only the nipping fall frosts develop the flavor of these slow-maturing roots, but the freezing cold of winter improves both texture and flavor.

In the selection of seed, there is only one variety of the real salsify to choose. Sometime we will want to try the perennial black salsify and Scolymus, or Spanish salsify, a much larger and more productive sort. For our first season, however, we might choose the small-rooted variety with the big name—the Mammoth Sandwich Island salsify, or oyster plant. I should simply name them vegetable oysters; it is the similarity of their flavor to oysters that makes them appetizing.

These roots, measuring rarely more than 2 or 3 inches across the root-crowns, have large seeds that are really fruits, long, gray and stick-like, so full of vitality that we may expect a healthy seedling for each fruit.

Parsnip seeds germinate rather slowly and have a very short vitality, only a year or two. For that reason, fresh seed should be secured each year, and plenty should be sown. The Hollow Crown is the best parsnip. Soaking the weak parsnip seed will hasten germination; and scattering the quick radish seeds along the furrow will keep the crust from hardening, and these robust plants will make early life easier for the frail parsnips. Seeding may be done just as early as the ground can be worked. In fitting the strip for seed-sowing, be careful to work the soil deeply and thoroughly enough to render it uniform and fine and to get rid of every stone, every obstacle to straight smooth-growing roots. With parsnips and salsify, especially, the harvest is settled before ever the seed is sown. As they work their way down, the roots will turn aside or branch at the least obstruction in the way. Sometimes a small stone has been found lodged between the forks of a vegetable oyster root. Rough uneven branched roots tell the story of careless, haphazard underground preparation; short stumpy roots show lack of deep working of the soil. When parsnips have a fair chance, they will sometimes push their way down thirty inches. The fibrous roots near the surface are needed for early feeding; but when the soil is properly and thoroughly prepared clear through, there will be few fibrous roots; we may be certain of long, smooth, tapering roots that well repay all the labor of preparation.

The general surface care given the entire root strip will be sufficient for the long-season roots, so far as it goes. A little nitrate of soda to start growth; continual surface tillage to keep down the weeds and to cover the bulging root-crowns and to conserve the moisture; thinning to provide plenty of room; thorough watering two or three times in a dry season; these are the requisites for healthy sturdy root growth. Supplement this with deepening tillage as these long roots try to stretch down. Till deeply for parsnips and salsify. There are no diseases, few enemies to prey on the beauty of the foliage or spoil the roots. When the hard frost has despoiled the garden's beauty, the long luxuriant green rows of parsnips and salsify are a sure satisfaction to the gardener.

After the first hard frost, a few roots may be dug; as the cold increases, the flavor will improve. They may be used as long as they can be dug. A part of the crop may be stored in moist sand in storehouse or cellar. So long as the roots do not shrivel, they make very good eating. The best parsnips and salsify, however, will be found in the ground after the long cold winter's seasoning.

They are a most satisfying spring surprise,—
ready for use just as soon as the snow has melted
over the row and the ground is thawed enough
to penetrate with the garden spade. At that time,
the flavor and texture are prime, a most appetizing change after the long winter diet of cellar-
stored roots. In the very early spring until
growth starts, the texture of these ground-stored
roots is crisp and firm and their flavor fresh and
fragrant. After the growth of new tops begins,
the roots lose flavor and soon become lean and
limp and tough and stringy, for the starch that
made crisp firm roots has gone into green tops.
Therefore, begin digging very early. Dig just
enough for one meal or what you intend to cook
immediately, as wilted roots are flavorless. Prepare them for cooking straightway. Salsify roots
become dark after peeling. As fast as they are
scrubbed, they should be placed in water to which
has been added a little vinegar and some flour.
That will keep them white.

These roots with the oyster flavor are especially
nutritious and healthful, even medicinal, a real
remedy for indigestion. The medicinal value is
said to be in the thick milky juice that exudes
from the surface as soon as the skin is broken.
This waste may be prevented by a sort of blanching, parboiling before peeling or scraping the
roots. Both of these varieties of roots may be
prepared in the same way. Merely scrub them

clean and put them into the cooker. Afterwards, whatever is necessary may be done. Some roots, like beets, have a thick heavy skin that slips off readily in cold water. Young carrots have scarcely a film of skin to be rubbed off. The skin of tender salsify roots is not much thicker; parsnips may need scraping. A stew of vegetable oysters is just as delicious as one made of the real bivalves and much more healthful. Both kinds of roots served whole in a sauce make a most appetizing stew; cut in two lengthwise, rolled in cracker crumbs and browned in butter, their own peculiar flavor adds much to the hearty breakfast for hungry country folks. In whatever way cooked or served, both of these long-season roots are palatable and nutritious, deserving a full share of room and attention in the home garden.

XXVI

PEAS

THE only all-important matter in the cultu.'e of garden peas is to grow an abundance of them; grow a succession of these meltingly sweet delicious legumes. Make sure of plenty of green peas with the new potatoes for Fourth of July dinner; keep them coming so long as it can be managed. Muggy midsummer weather is sometimes hard on peas. Mildew and lice may then attack the leaves; and blight may injure leaf and stalk and pod. In spite of all these hot-weather difficulties, in an ordinary season in central New York climate, with intelligent care, the gardener may succeed in producing plenty of peas from early July even until frost has come. The sweetest, tenderest, most delicate-flavored peas and the biggest crops are grown in the cool fresh air of spring and early summer. Consequently an abundant supply should be provided for that most favorable time. Grow all that the family can use. In each sowing this means an allowance of at least 15 feet to each one at the home table; plan for some panfuls of the plump pods to pass on to the gardenless neighbors; and in addition,

allow for a sufficient supply for canning in the
early sowings. Begin putting in peas as soon as
the ground is workable and continue sowing every
ten days until midsummer. Not one pod need be
wasted. (Plate VII.) Whatever the season,
whatever the variety, there are never too many
garden peas.

For the kitchen-garden there is a variety of
edible peas just suited to each season. After a
little experience, every gardener will have special
favorites. For the present, let us choose a quick-
maturing dwarf variety like First of All or Nott's
Excelsior for the first sowing. Very soon afterwards, put in some long rows of the taller-growing
varieties like Prosperity, an excellent tall sort for
early sowing. When seeded at the same time as
the First of All, their bigger growth delays maturity long enough so that, soon after the First of
Alls are gone, the Prosperitys are ready with an
abundance of large tender peas of most delicate
flavor. For the main crop sow the five-foot tall,
deeply rooted Telephones. They, in their turn,
will furnish a lot of big luscious-sweet peas. The
heavy-growing and heavy-cropping Champion of
England deserves the same honor in America as
a long-time first favorite. When kept in healthy
growth, this sturdy, heat-resisting, blight-defying,
wrinkled variety will provide a bountiful supply
of delicious peas of marrow-rich flavor, until
stopped by the frost. One more variety might well

be suggested,—Horsford Market Garden. These
peas are grown by the acres for commercial
canning; and their sturdy self-supporting growth
and prodigious crop of plump pods, filled full of
tender full-flavored peas, are equally satisfactory
when raised in the home garden, especially for
canning. Depending on a surplus from the successional sowings is risking the winter supply of
this indispensable delicacy. Put in plenty of
Horsford Market Garden peas; put them in
early; and, when they are just prime, put the
entire crop into glass jars and store them away
in a cool dark cellar. However many we may
sow, when grown properly and gathered at just
the right time, there will never be any surplus of
garden peas. We must be forehanded and provide
for green peas the year around.

Garden peas will grow almost anywhere, in
almost any kind of soil, with almost any care.
However, the success at the harvest will be in
proportion to the intelligent care with reference
to soil, seed and sowing, and persistent later
attention. Peas grow best in an open sandy loam.
For any soil to be open or porous, there must be
provided plenty of humus, the warp of the soil.
This material lightens and aërates the soil; and,
if the bottom-drainage has been looked after,
assures the gardener of completely drained soil.
The heavier the texture, the more necessary is
humus and the larger the quantity needed. Plenty

of humus prevents hard packing of the soil during the winter months and, therefore, ensures rapid upper soil drainage and drying in the early spring; and that, almost of itself, makes a quick soil. This soil fiber is especially necessary for peas. Too rich or fertile soil hinders the maturity of early peas. As with all legumes, rich soil for early peas tends to produce mainly vine instead of pods. At any event, fruitage is sure to be delayed. For the earliest sowings, light stalk growth is desired and only one full flowering is expected. To bring about limited growth of stalk with abundant bloom and a quickly developing plentiful harvest, a light soil is needed, one that is not too rich. Later in the season, with varieties that naturally produce big growth, a richer heavier soil serves excellently. At that time of slower growth, large tops are needed for the production of big crops, to induce continued blossoming and steady formation of pods. The summer-grown peas need also a deep rooting system for the sustenance of healthy productive growth in midseason heat. Therefore, open, quick, sandy soil is best for early peas; richer more retentive loams, for later sowings.

Some care with reference to seed is necessary. Peas are peculiarly liable to the attacks of the pea-weevil. When we produce our own seed from our own chosen varieties, we shall store the seed with the same care given the corn, in air-tight receptacles, providing for riddance of the weevils with carbon-bisulfide. Experiments with buggy peas have made clear the importance of this precaution. While weevil-less peas sprouted perfectly, the germination of buggy peas, under the same conditions, was at best only a quarter of those tested. In some trials, only one seed out of fifty sprouted. Whether purchased or raised in the home garden, the seed must be treated with carbon-bisulfide while in moth-proof containers and kept from the air until planted.

As to the time of planting peas, all the gardeners and garden books to the contrary, it does not pay to put in peas or any other seed when the ground is nearly freezing-cold and soaking-wet. Wait, instead, until the spring sunshine has warmed the air, and the ground has drained enough so that the lumps crumble easily beneath the drag teeth. Then, put in the First of Alls in the more open sandy strip. Lay out double rows, 2 feet apart, at least for early peas; 3 feet, anyway, for later sowings. In the double rows, allow 6 or 8 inches, the width of the hook between the sowings for cultivating. Sow the early peas in a furrow, nearly 4 inches deep; the later peas at least an inch lower to provide for moisture for germination and to aid deeper rooting in hot weather. Place the early slighter growing varieties ten seeds to the foot; the later, bigger, branching sorts need more room, say 3 or 4 inches.

To protect the seeds from the cutworms, tobacco dust in the furrow is reliable. Firming is always, necessary to rapid germination; but, with these deep-sown seeds that must take time to reach the surface, it may also be necessary to scratch the surface of the rows with rake or hook to prevent cracking. With such care as to seed and sowing, on the gardener's part, the spring weather will do the remainder; and, in a surprisingly short time, long even rows of fresh green sprouts in the bare garden will be the first satisfying hope of a garden.

Later attention for garden peas is nearly the same as for all vegetables. Strange as it may seem after what has just been said concerning too-fertile soils, garden peas should have a food stimulant to start growth. Although peas, like all leguminous plants, are nitrogen-gatherers, capable of using atmospheric nitrogen, they do not seem able to make ready use of soil nitrogen in starting growth rapidly. Unless our peas follow some other legume—and that is against the frugal and health-providing rotation rule—they should have one application of nitrate of soda, just as growth begins. Afterwards, the peas will grow rapidly and, as they grow, breathe in this growth stimulant from the air, storing it away in their nitrogen nodules, enough and to spare.

After growth has fairly begun, the healthy vines will need support of some sort. The First of

Alls might be left to themselves, but they will mature quicker and produce a bigger harvest if they are at least brushed. They are more attractive if kept upright with narrow chicken-wire. All the later varieties should be supported with this woven wire. Use a width to fit the natural growth; stretch it tightly between the single rows, holding it firmly in place with stout stakes driven' at the ends of the rows and wherever needed to prevent sagging. As soon as the peas begin to bend the least bit, turn them towards the wire netting, as they are cultivated. Either the hoe or the plow-point of the wheel cultivator will easily turn an even furrow on both sides of the green rows. Turning the soil towards the peas or hilling them does more than to keep them growing upright. This is an especial advantage with the later sowings, protecting them from the surface heat and making it possible for the roots to reach more moisture when most needed. An extra supply of water may be necessary if the season is very dry. In that event, using the same cultivator point, make a little furrow or trench along the rows. Fill it full with water from the hose; and, after the water is entirely absorbed, turn another furrow of soil over the "irrigation" trench and cover that with some sort of strawy mulch. Usually, one watering of that thorough kind will carry the peas safely through a dry season and ensure the harvest.

Plant-lice attacking the garden pea may be controlled by a thorough hosing and then stirring the top soil. If this is not effective, use a soap solution in a spray. Thorough surface tillage is a good preventive of disease, but a bordeaux spray may be necessary.

Early July comes soon; and then new peas and new potatoes and spring lamb. However great the skill and care in their production, garden peas are tough and flavorless unless they are gathered when just right. Pick the peas while the pods are not quite full, while they are still a fresh green. Gather all that are ready at each inspection. Gather the peas early in the morning, before the heated air has wilted the pods; wilted peas are flavorless. Put the pods where it is cool until time for shelling. If they are wilted, a plunge into cold water restores the crispness and the flavor partially. Whether to be eaten immediately or canned, if the delicacy of the fresh flavor is to be retained, they must be cooked straightway after shelling. With garden peas more than any other vegetable, the word is straight from the garden, in the early morning, to the cooker or the can. With care to pick them before they are over-ripe, while the pods are fresh and crisp, and then care in not allowing them to wilt before cooking, we may always depend on peas that are meltingly tender and deliciously sweet, from the first picking until frost has gathered the last mess.

XXVII

POTATOES

For potatoes the soil should be rich and deep and free from stones. The seed potatoes should be dropped uncut, placing them in rows 3 feet apart with 30 inches between the hills. Extra fertilizer may be added, but too much nutriment means big tubers with coarse watery texture and diluted flavor. Poor top growth indicates lack of fertilizer, while over-feeding is shown by big coarse over-heavy tops. The depth of covering on the potatoes does not matter much so far as growth is concerned, but putting about 4 inches below the surface will help to insure moisture. Hilled potatoes, especially on a slope, wash more in a heavy rain and the bare potatoes are exposed to sun-burn. Place the seed deep enough for nearly level cultivation.

Start ordinary cultivation immediately. This will conserve the moisture, prepare the food and keep the weeds down. Rain is needed at first, as after each spring rain new tubers form. After this, dry weather is just as necessary, as rain causes too many potatoes to set and the mature tubers will be small. Continued rain will cause

187

the potatoes to be coarse in texture and of poor flavor and the entire crop may rot.

Spraying is a necessary protection against potato diseases and insects. Bordeaux mixture may be used, together with paris green.

In digging potatoes, choose clear dry cool weather. Turn them out to the surface, leaving them to dry off. If the ground is wet and sticky, the soil will not shake clear, the potatoes will be unpleasant to handle, and they are likely to rot. If the weather is hot and muggy, leave the potatoes on the ground, protecting them from the sun. When the potatoes are dry and clean, store in bins in a cool dry cellar with plenty of fresh air and protection from light.

XXVIII

RADISHES

The tiny scarlet radish is a crisp spring relish,
its color a real garnish. French Breakfast is
the kind to choose. These piquant relishes may
have a place in the earliest sowing in the hotbed
and in the garden lettuce bed. Grow the tiny
roots among the head lettuce, in the row of cabbages or cauliflower. Sow them in the furrow
with any slow-germinating seed, like carrots or
parsnips. The big seeds are full of life and germinate quickly. The bigger the seeds, the stronger
the vitality, the more vigorous and rapid the
growth. Tillage along the rows may start sooner
because of the radishes. These roots will have
the first chance at the soil food. Being surface
feeders, we may hurry them with a bit of nitrate
of soda, as we stir the soil. They will be fully
matured and out of the way before the space is
needed for the slower growing plants. They will
thrive almost anywhere; but the best place for
crisp radishes, and they must grow with a snap, if
they are to be crisp and their biting flavor just
mild enough, is a rich early sandy strip. Sandy
soil seems to safeguard the radishes from their

sole enemy, the root-maggot. Sow them, a few at a time, until warm weather. They will be ready to pull in less than a month. Their fresh red color and biting taste are a part of early spring. A heaped plate of the tiny red roots with the green tops for a garnish will be hunger sauce for the meal. Their bit of red and pungent taste are an addition to any salad.

XXIX

SPINACH

As now developed, this favorite pot-herb, under proper conditions, may be made to produce tender greens the whole season through, by sowing at intervals. It is usually sown very early in the spring, and again in the fall to be wintered over for the next spring's use. By planting a heat-resisting variety and by care in selection of cool, rich, moist soil, it may be grown with real success even in midsummer. In the choice of varieties, if the gardener wishes to try two sorts, there is one especially intended for fall sowing. Thick Leaved spinach produces large crumpled leaves of excellent quality and is very hardy. The so-called New Zealand spinach is not really a spinach. It withstands heat much better than any true spinach and, for that reason, is coming into popular use for midsummer greens. The plants grow tall and are branched, yielding a continual supply of quite palatable leaves. Long Season is an all-around satisfactory variety that, while at its best in the spring, will do well with the proper attention at any time of the year in an ordinary season. In a hot dry season, no skill or care seems always

191

equal to good spinach in midsummer. In a cool moist summer, however, or when grown in a cool moist shady spot, even in a dry year Long Season is almost always satisfactory. This spinach will grow luxuriantly in early spring; it continues to provide palatable greens in midsummer; and, sown again in September, will make growth sturdy enough to weather the winter, even in central New York climate, and be ready with fresh greens in the very early spring. It may grow a little more slowly, but it puts all its vigor into leaf-making. It has very short stems; is nearly all foliage; it is the slowest variety to go to seed. Long Season spinach is perfect, in its rich dark color and thick tender leaves, delicate enough for salad.

The cultivation of lettuce and spinach is much alike. The conditions favorable to the growth of big tender-crisp heads of lettuce will also produce broad, rich green, succulent spinach plants. However, lettuce will grow on lean soil; but if spinach is sown in poor sterile soil, the old tendency will assert itself and, for our best care, there will only be stunted foliage and almost immediate growth of stalk; the plants will merely run to seed. Even after luxuriant foliage growth has already been made, when stalk growth begins, the leaves always lose their tender succulence and become tough and bitter. The poorer the soil, the quicker this plant goes to seed; the

poorer the harvest of greens. Spinach must have
rich soil to feed on. The more luxuriant the
growth, the more delicious are the greens. Choose
the richest strip in the garden, perhaps where
the Champion of England peas were the season
before, or the lima beans. Make it richer by an
application of commercial fertilizer when the
strip is fitted for sowing. Then sow Long Season spinach while the ground is cool and moist.
After seeding, furnish still more of the necessary
foliage food in a sprinkle of nitrate along the
rows; continue this magical growth stimulant
every few days; and the gardener may be certain
of an early crop of the tenderest most appetizing
greens ever eaten. No other plant, not even lettuce, responds so surprisingly to nitrogen.
Nitrate of soda more than trebles the ordinary
size, producing great plants nearly a foot across,
just covering the surface with their big leaves.

Spinach seed is less vigorous than lettuce. We
need to sow it more thickly. Otherwise, treat it
like lettuce. Put the rows a foot apart; or sow it
in double rows, leaving 2 feet, anyway, between
the pairs of rows. Unless you decide to try New
Zealand spinach for the midsummer crop, put in
another sowing of Long Season, in two weeks or
more. Choose the dampest, coolest, shadiest spot,
maybe between the rows of tall beans or in the
shade of the corn. Then, in September, sow again
for the early spring greens. Do not use any more

than one application of nitrogen for the fall sowing. The plants should be sturdy enough by cold
weather to carry over safely.

In mild climates, the spinach is left uncovered.
In a climate like that of central New York, however, the plants should be protected by 3 or 4
inches of leaves or straw. If the snow comes
heavily, provided the spinach has been sown in a
sheltered place, away from the sweep of the wind,
merely the snow cover is the very best protection.

When we consider the spinach harvest, we shall
hope for a cool moist season. In a really dry year,
nothing seems to prevent spinach from running to
seed. A season with abundant sunshine and dry
weather is almost fatal to a good harvest of spinach, except the very early crop. Whatever the
season, it is always worth the trial. The proper
start has been made in rich soil. Follow it up
with frequent surface tillage. If a dry spell
threatens, give the spinach row a thorough soaking often. Do everything to bring about quick
growth.

There may be difficulty with the leaf-miner and,
sometimes, with the flea-beetle. Usually, tobacco
is sufficient to keep the plants free from their
ravages. Keep the garden border clear of lamb's
quarters, on which the miners feed. Fungus diseases do not seem to trouble the home-garden
spinach. It is good, however, for the promotion
of the plant health, to treat the spinach strip with

VIII.—Good Tomatoes Supported on a Wire Fence.

a mixture of flowers of sulfur with the air-slaked lime used for the entire garden. With intelligent care in the soil and tillage and plenty of water, despite the season the gardener may expect a crop of spinach.

Home-garden spinach is not much like market spinach. Keep on stirring the surface and supplying water, and let the plants grow as big as they will, so long as the center shows no sign of opening out for the stalk. They are ready for greens as soon as they are the size of your hand. Pull the biggest plants, along the rows, thus making room for bigger growth. Pull them, root and all, while crisp with early morning dew; shake off the soil, discarding any injured or mined leaves, and trim off the root ends. Then they are ready for washing; and the best place, in fair weather, for cleaning greens and all kinds of vegetables is at the sill-cock or by the well or the open trough. Plunge them into fresh water until no sign of grit is found at the bottom of the pan. Do not allow them to wilt. Leave them down cellar or in some other cool place until dinner time. They are so succulent, they will need no extra water in the pan when cooking. Merely pack the big tender bunches of green into the biggest pan, turning them as they wilt. These thick tender leaves are so juicy that they shrink amazingly when put into the pan; they are so rich in spinach flavor that they may be served

together with beet or any other mild-flavored
greens. When served alone, chop them a bit in
the pan with the turning knife; add plenty of
butter and salt; pack them into a mound; and
slice or grate over the top hard boiled eggs. For
variety, use thin slices of bacon for a garnish.
These spring greens are health-giving and delicious. Spinach is better than any spring medi-
cine. Whatever is left from the greens may be
sifted into a cream soup. Try some of these big
tender leaves in a salad with some mild flavored
plant like lettuce. Be sure to can all that may be
spared. Canned spinach is a delicious surprise,
when used the first winter. To put away for
winter, prepare just the same as for the table.
When cooked and seasoned, pack into the glass
jars, without adding water, and sterilize immediately. Spinach, like asparagus and all very
tender-textured plants, is much better sterilized
in a pressure canner. By that quicker method, the
texture is softened less and the greens are better.
Whatever the process, as soon as they are ren-
dered sterile, put the jars away in the cool dark
cellar and use them all before spring.

XXX

TOMATOES AND EGGPLANTS

OF all the fruits of the garden, none is used in so many ways or serves so many purposes as the tomato. It is indispensable in the successful practice of the culinary art. In salad and in sauce, for seasoning and for soup, for conserves, for pickles, in almost every kind of cooking, in preserving and pickling and spicing and flavoring, the cook must have an endless supply of tomatoes. They are also a joy in the growing. At the harvest, nothing brings more delight to the gardener than the first bright-colored, smooth-skinned, fragrant tomatoes, glowing rich-red against the dark leaves.

In planning, one must provide, at least, for an early and a main crop. The Earliana might be suggested for the earliest sort. The Stone has proven its reliability for the main crop. It is sturdy and healthy in growth, producing large crops of smooth-skinned firm-fleshed fine-flavored fruit. The smooth thick skin of the Stone tomato makes it the best kind for canning whole. Tenderloin is especially liked because of its compact meaty texture, deep red clear to the heart. This

197

variety is also robust and very prolific. Put in a few plants of Earliana for the first salad. Then depend on the heavier-meated more solid Stone and Tenderloin for canning and pickling and spicing, as well as for fresh slicing for salad.

We may start the tomatoes from the seed. The gardener who knows how to grow healthy robust celery plants will easily succeed in producing perfect tomatoes. The soil that is suitable to start celery is just adapted for tomatoes. The same care will be needed to keep the seedlings growing sturdily, an even supply of moisture, plenty of fresh air and light, and care in surface tillage as the young plants develop. Transplanting from flat to coldframe will prevent leggy spindling growth and ensure stocky plants with healthy dark green leaves. The time for sowing tomato seed, in a climate like central New York, is St. Patrick's day. Sow the seeds in flats or hotbed; and be sure to transplant at least once, twice is better, before setting in the open ground. In vast fields where great crops of tomatoes are grown to supply the canning factories, much less care and attention are necessarily given; but, for the home garden, when the aim is early, healthy, robust plants, the extra trouble pays well. If the seeds are sown about the seventeenth of March, by the middle of April the seedlings will be ready for their first transplanting; move them as soon as the first true leaves appear. Then the sturdiest,

those that are 1½ or 2 inches tall, should be removed to fresh soil, giving them at least 2 inches
of room. In another three weeks, or whenever the
plants seem to crowd, they are ready for the last
move until garden setting. This time, double the
space is allowed for growth; or better still, put
the plants into separate containers, berry-boxes,
paper pots, or unsoldered tin can bands. The
plants may now remain to become stocky and
strong and to produce a big bunch of fibrous roots.
Ten days after corn planting is tomato-setting
time. That is usually just after Decoration Day,
not before, because a late frost seems to threaten
just then. Perhaps it was decided to buy the
plants this year. Then arrange with a reliable
market-gardener who will furnish plants true to
name. Select the plants yourself, the kind you
would like to grow, stocky, strong, healthy, dark
foliaged specimens.

Tomatoes will grow in almost any kind of soil;
the finest specimens and the largest yields have
been produced in favorable seasons in all types
of soil. The proper location of the tomato strip,
however, with reference both to soil and to protection from frost, will lengthen the season at both
ends and increase the yield and improve the quality of the product. A rich sandy soil is ideal for
tomatoes. Deep moist loams will produce big
growth of plants; but a quick soil is most important, especially for the early varieties, in an

ordinary season in a central New York climate. A sandy soil, well-drained, may be made suitable by the incorporation of plenty of the proper fertilizer; an abundance of humus and completely rotted manure in the fall preparation; a quickly available commercial fertilizer rich in potash in the spring; and a bit of stimulating nitrate to start growth at planting time. These are ideal soil conditions for tomatoes. A strip of rich loam at the sheltered base of the orchard slope has produced excellent crops of tomatoes; but, usually, the frost has caught about half the crop before they began to ripen. A sandy leaner strip on an upland slope brought a complete harvest. The plants did not make such lusty growth as those over-fed in the rich strip of loam at the hill-bottom; perhaps the tomatoes were not so large and the yield was not so great; but the fruit was more uniform and firmer in texture, and nearly the entire crop ripened because of the lengthened season. The frost that burned the plants in the rich garden strip sheltered from the wind left the breeze-swept upland strip untouched.

Let us put some of the tomato plants on the upland slope and some on the rich loam in the garden. The Earlianas would do especially well in the garden strip and the tomatoes would be handy for the first salads. Wherever the plants are set, whatever the variety, tomatoes should always be grown in hills, in the home garden, since we wish to produce the best possible fruit. The arrangement of the hills will be in rows, at least 4 feet apart. The distance between the plants will depend on the method of growth and support. When trimmed to only one or two stalks and trained to stakes, 2 feet will be room enough. If the plants are unpruned and supported on frames, twice as much room will be needed. If we try staking the plants, allow 4 feet between rows and 2 feet between hills. Prepare the hills deep and broad, making the soil loose and fine. At the bottom of the hill, put a small fire-shovelful of the heat-producing stimulating hen-manure. Cover the manure well; set the plant with the wet soil adhering to the bunch of roots; firm carefully as the hole is filled; scatter a little tobacco near the surface to keep the cutworms away. Soak each hill thoroughly after the plants are set; and then give them one application of sodium nitrate. Too much nitrate produces heavy useless foliage and endless stalk growth that keeps on stretching out, in spite of persistent nipping. Too much nitrogen results in a smaller yield, and the fruit is soft-textured and tends to rot. Give each hill one tablespoonful scattered over a two-foot space or applied in a solution with the sprinkling pot. Then go over the entire strip with the hook to work in the nitrate and, at the same time, form the water-conserving dust mulch. Unless some cloudy weather follows the plant setting, it will be necessary to provide some sort of shade for a few days, in the hottest part. After the roots get a grip on the soil and begin to make use of the supplies of food and moisture, the plants should make steady healthy growth.

If the growing tomatoes remain healthy, the further care during the season will be simple. Regular tillage is of course necessary. Plenty of water must be supplied if the season is hot and the ground becomes dry. For the best results, the plants will need support and pruning. In large fields, tomato vines are usually left un-pruned and prone upon the ground; but unsup-ported plants are sure to lose quite a good deal of the harvest, through poor development and be-cause of rot. While this method may be followed, on account of the great expense of extra labor in-volved, where great quantities are grown, the home gardener will spare no pains or labor that may contribute towards a prize harvest. Some-times racks are used; and the plants are pruned only slightly.

We have decided to stake our tomatoes and prune them to a single main stem, or tie the one stem to a wire screen (Plate VIII). Staking and pruning may lessen the size of the crop; but it will improve the appearance of the tomato strip; the plants are healthier and more easily cared for; the fruit is firmer and more uni-form and of better quality; maturity is earlier and a much larger proportion of the tomatoes ripen. Put in stout 8-foot stakes, soon after setting, driving in firmly. Tie the young plants, soon after, using a soft jute string; take care to bring the loop around beneath the leaf node, so that the plants will not slip and sag. As soon as the plants are staked, or when new growth starts, the pruning begins. Perhaps the gardener will decide to allow two branches to develop on the main stem. Then pinch out all other lateral buds, just as growth starts. The fruit stems will be in no danger, for they appear on the opposite side of the branch, between the leaves. Do not allow the branch to grow. Pruning large branches wastes plant vigor; sometimes the bleeding actually kills the plant. Watch closely and pinch out new growth; and watch also for the suckers that usually appear soon after pruning begins. They waste the vitality of the main plant that is to produce the harvest. After blooming begins, the gardener may hasten the ripening of the much prized first tomatoes by nipping off a part of the buds. Later on in the season, after plenty of fruit has formed, the vine ends may be pinched and thus growth and blossoming stopped and the entire vigor of the plant turned to maturing and ripening the fruit. In this way, by pruning or controlling and directing growth and by furnishing support, health is more perfectly assured and much finer tomatoes are produced. This method of growing tomatoes makes it possible, also, to find room for them in the smallest kind of a back-yard garden.

The best prevention of disease is always steady healthy growth. Spraying with bordeaux mixture is the best remedy for most tomato diseases. Tobacco dust sifted over the leaves will keep away flea-beetles and plant-lice.

No harvest is quite so interesting in anticipation as the tomato harvest. As the biggest fruits turn light and then begin to color, they must have plenty of sunshine to give them rich color and fine flavor. Cut out overshadowing leaves and turn the branches toward the light. Provide water when necessary and keep the surface stirred. Pinch the vine ends and so turn all the vitality toward final development and ripening. The big clumps may become so heavy that they may need tying to the stake to keep them from breaking down. Watch out, ready for the last bit of care here and there, and soon the gardener will be gathering big basketfuls of luscious red tomatoes.

Eggplants

The cultivation of eggplant is practically the same as for the tomato, except we must bear in mind that it is a hot-season plant. The eggplant needs a long season and warm, loose, fairly dry, loamy soil. To extend the time of growth usually allowed by our central New York climate, the plants are started under glass. Six or eight inches of thrifty stocky growth will make them ready for the open garden. It is an advantage to handle the plants twice in pots before finally setting them where they are to mature. This lessens the danger of checking the growth. Find a warm sunny strip of soil, not so moist as ground suited to the early peas. Make it rich and fit the same as for the tomato, putting extra heat-producing fertilizer below the plants. Growth must proceed immediately after transplanting and continue unchecked until the fruit is ready to be gathered. Care must be given to cultivation.

Sometimes the insects that trouble the tomatoes will attack the eggplants, but usually the growth will be healthy. Keep the surface well tilled; use tobacco dust against the flea-beetles, and soon the blossoms begin to show. As the fruits develop, staking will help to keep them upright. When the eggs are only a third grown, 6 inches or even less, they are ready for frying. From then until they are beginning to ripen, these southern vegetables furnish an appetizing variety for the table.

The little garden book is ended. I hope it contains good advice; certainly the statements are born of experience. I trust, also, that it will encourage sentiment for real gardens, and that it will recall many memories.

A flash of memory brings a glimpse of the home

of a childhood friend. A low doorstep opens
level with the worn stone and right by the side
door a stately elm casts its widespreading shade.
The grass-grown pebble walk leads out through
the flower-garden to the place of adventure.
Honeysuckles grow in sweet clumps here and
there in the tall grass along the path; the flowering almonds are fragrant with their tiny rose-like
blossoms; "pineys" rich and red shed their soft
petals under our feet. Beyond is the broken
bit of "teetering" plank across the narrow dry
gully in front of the gate. With the creak of the
rusty hinges began childhood's adventure,—the
orchard where the gilliflowers grew and the rus-
sets, and where we played as we devoured the
luscious strawberry apples, juicy and ripe. Nothing but the supper call could bring us back to
prosaic life again. New worlds open, old times
come again with the lotus scent, the flash of color
of the flowers, and the old gardens.

The breeze goes down towards the end of a quiet
day. The dew brings close the scent of growing
things, and whiff of lavender. Now I see grand-
mother's cool shuttered room and the sweet-
smelling linen in the depths of the old chest of
drawers, and a low weather-grayed homestead on
the slope of the hill, in the wide unmown door-
yard. Near the angle of the woodshed ell stands
the open trough, its cool gurgling water overflow-
ing the moss-streaked battered sides. Nearby on

the bench is the row of shining milk-pails turned up to the sun, the gourd dipper at hand for a drink. On the long narrow porch beneath the slope of the roof, the splint-back rocker with its red-moreen cover and its plump feather cushion invites repose. It is a step from the porch to the ground. On either side of the wide flag doorstone always, year after year, were the China asters. The forget-me-nots crept close to the walk, with the stepping-stones nearly buried by the tread of many years. By the gateway, at the turn of the path toward the barns, was a mountain ash; and along the picket fence the lilacs grew.

INDEX

Printed in the United States
142985LV00013B/93/P